THE MODERN SAMURAI SOCIETY

THE MODERN SAMURAI SOCIETY

Duty and Dependence in CONTEMPORARY JAPAN

MITSUYUKI MASATSUGU

 American Management Associations

Library of Congress Cataloging in Publication Data

Masatsugu, Mitsuyuki.
   The modern samurai society.

   Includes index.
     1. Japan—Social conditions. 2. National character-
istics, Japanese. 3. Management. I. Title.
HN723.M29   306'.0952   81-69363
ISBN 0-8144-5730-4   AACR2

© 1982 AMACOM Book Division
American Management Associations, New York.

First Printing

to

Kiyoko

in appreciation of
three decades of partnership

PREFACE

Today, many Japanese jet out of their native islands and go abroad. Almost every one of them is, without notice, snapshotted from unexpected angles, at the corner of a thriving street or in front of an historical landmark. The next morning, or even a few hours later on the same day, the photo is printed on glossy paper and is presented forcibly to the Japanese visitor for sale.

To be sure, his curiosity compels him to peep into the picture and meet himself. With pleasure or surprise, or even a bit of sorrow, he discovers from the profile a person he has not been aware of and says, "Oh, no, is this me? What a unique human being I am!" Beyond expectation, he experiences genuine emotion about himself.

The nation as a whole is so as well. Until the people are exposed to themselves objectively, they do not know who they are. The Japanese have lived happily together for centuries, speaking one language and maintaining their homogeneity within the narrow island country. Their insularity has created such distinctive cultural characteristics that people throughout the world have claimed that Japanese thought and culture is the most enigmatic and paradoxical of all national traditions. The major reason is that for many years the culture was never truly exposed to foreigners.

Recently, however, the Japanese have been brought onto the world stage by the frenzied activities of journalists. Many views of Japan have been put forward by foreign scholars and writers, who have begun to expose the nation to the eyes of the world.

Japan's successful struggle in the international economy has attracted particular attention. As a result, the Japanese people are becoming aware of themselves for the first time and Japan is now being flooded with study missions from both developed and developing countries.

Nevertheless, the reticence of the Japanese people would never allow them to express themselves fully, so the descriptions of Japan always come from foreigners. Although the freshness of foreigners' eyes often leads to new discoveries, their analyses are inevitably made from outside angles. Though not incorrect, their portrayal is nonetheless an outsider's point of view.

For instance, they are likely to uphold the techniques of quality control in the production lines as the key to Japan's economic achievement without truly understanding what is behind the techniques. Or they are likely to point out "Japan Incorporated" as the successful manipulator of the economy, and the lifetime employment system of Japanese management as the source of the people's loyalty and enthusiasm, without detecting the cultural traits supporting such systems.

The truth is that the success of such unique Japanese systems as lifetime employment, seniority-based promotion, and the QC circle lies in the fact that Japanese management has been able to tactfully incorporate into them two critical features of Japanese culture: "diligence" *(kimben)*, the duty of an agricultural race; and "dependence" *(amae)*, the fundamental characteristic of Japanese society. This point has never been sufficiently understood by foreigners—nor has it ever been explored on the public stage by the Japanese people themselves.

This very fact is what compelled me to write about Japan and Japanese industry in English. Instead of taking an academic approach to the subject, I have adopted an historical approach by presenting real-life examples and a logical analysis of what makes the Japanese people and Japanese management tick. I have tried hard not to be biased by my patriotism. My past experiences in working with Americans as an adviser on Japanese personnel, in working as a samurai for a large Japanese company, and in working with Europeans and other nationalities on the staff of the United Nations have greatly helped me keep my writing unbiased.

This book is an honest and, I hope, unambiguous presentation from a Japanese to non-Japanese. It would be my great pleasure if the book assisted readers in learning more about the Japanese people and Japanese management.

In writing the book, I was assisted by Jeffrey R. Hunter and by Yoshie Masatsugu, who translated some of my own special materials. Their dedicated service expedited my work, and I wish to express my thanks for their strenuous efforts. I am also indebted to Robert A. Kaplan, who gave me constant encouragement, and to Louise Marinis and other members of the American Management Associations who kindly rendered their valuable services in the production of the manuscript.

Mitsuyuki Masatsugu
July 1981

CONTENTS

1

ISOLATION SPAWNED THE CULTURE

The geographic factor of greatest importance in molding the culture of Japan has been its isolation.

Like Italy, Japan is a mountainous country, and like Britain, Japan is an island country—the four main islands and numerous smaller ones are all surrounded by the sea. In total area Japan is about as large as the state of California. The straits between western Japan and Korea, the nearest continental land, are over 100 miles apart, many times the width of the Straits of Dover, the narrowest point between Britain and continental Europe. And some 500 miles of open sea stretch between Japan and China. In the days of primitive navigation, these water barriers were quite broad and made Japan the most isolated country of large population in the world. This geographic isolation has led the Japanese to develop extremely distinctive national traits.

The origins of the Japanese people have never been traced to the satisfaction of scholars. The first inhabitants of the islands seem to have been the ancestors of the modern Ainu, who came from the north, where the climate is severely cold. According to historians, the Ainu were a tribal group which branched off from the white race at such an early time that not all the characteristics of Caucasian stock had as yet developed. This race might once have inhabited all of Japan, but in many ways its culture was inferior to that of the early Mongoloid peoples, who came to Japan from the Chinese continent. Accordingly, the Ainu were gradually pushed northward, and they now exist only as a vanishing people in the remote sections of Hokkaido and in the small islands in the north. However, blood of the Ainu surely remains in the Japanese people of today.

Linguists suggest that there is a strong oceanic and Malaysian strain in the Japanese race. It is a popular theory that oceanic races arrived in Japan from the south by way of Formosa (Taiwan) and the Ryukyu (Okinawa) Islands. At any rate, the ancestors of the Japanese people were an exquisite mixture of unneighborly races that arrived from the north, the west, and the south—quite contrasting areas. (See Figure 1.) Thus it is a plausible proposition that the nature-loving character of the Japanese people, manifested in the art of flower arrangement, landscape gardening, and the like, was brought in from the north and that the pugnacious temperament, evidenced in so much warfare, was inherited from the south. A unique and exclusive culture, which sometimes strikes foreigners as contradictory today, was thus spawned over thousands of years within the isolated Japanese islands.

The state of virtual isolation affected the culture in many ways. First of all, it produced a homogeneous union of people, whose cohesiveness led to monarchy as early as the seventh century. Or it may be put the other way around: isolation forced the people to be unified and unification created a strong cohesiveness among the Japanese people. In any case, cohesiveness has been a basic characteristic of the Japanese nation and its culture ever since.

According to the old Chinese concept of sovereignty, the monarch enjoyed the "mandate of Heaven," but only so long as he was virtuous. If he lacked sovereign virtue, he could be overthrown by Heaven. This was, in Chinese history, often accepted as the justification for a political rebellion. In fact, both China and Korea were ruled by several dynasties which were

Figure 1. Presumed migration routes to Japan in early times.

overthrown one after another. In Japan, by contrast, although there have been countless instances of civil strife and warfare, there has been only one Imperial dynasty. Speaking only one language and acting essentially as one race, the Japanese people are completely unified.

In the course of time, the people enclosed in the isolated areas—later to become overcrowded—developed a strong competitive spirit, and keen competition has been taking place among them ever since. Thus the observation that Japan is not a society of competition but rather a society of consensus is not 100 percent accurate. The Japanese are among the most competitive people in the world; otherwise they could not have achieved their recent economic successes. Consensus was established to keep the society cohesive and to control excessive competition, which would cause friction and make tireless rivals of the people in the isolated areas. So the comment that Japan is a society of consensus is only one side of the story.

It is proved in Japan's ancient history that every feudal lord with his samurai (subordinates) was intensely competitive with neighboring lords and was always prepared for any unexpected challenge from others. Even today, despite the waves of social criticism, intense competition continues in the renewed system of scholastic examinations. A fanatic "examination war" is going on among high school students who wish to enter prestigious universities in order to ensure advantageous future careers. In no other country is the learning fever of the youngsters described as akin to war. It should also be noted that the competition among Japanese commercial enterprises is very fierce in their particular battlefield, the marketplace. This flaming competitive spirit certainly played a large part in building up the Japanese industries of today.

In the early centuries, knowing the nature of the people, the ruling class of Japan searched for a balanced social ideal that would keep the people in harmony and prevent the tragic outcomes of excessive competition. When the centralized state was established by Prince Shotoku in A.D. 604, after the conflicts among various clans had ended, *wa* (concord) was stressed as the most important principle of the community. Prince Shotoku emphasized harmonious human relations and prescribed "concord" in the first article of the Seventeen Article Constitution. This was the first piece of legislation in Japan, and is, so to speak, its Magna Carta.

Some observers have noted that the Japanese people possess an excitable and volatile temperament and suggest that the traditional code of manners was adopted as an essential check on the social disorder that could follow from the free exercise of hereditary emotion. It is a fact that *wa*, a harmonious concord, has been the highest ideal of the nation since Prince Shotoku proclaimed the constitution. Those who visit a company president's office or a main office of a factory in Japan very often find a calligraphic *wa* in a frame hanging on the wall.

This suggests that the traditional code of *wa* has not come naturally to the Japanese—that the people need a constant reminder of their social ideal. Their impassive attitude and reserved manner toward others in an effort to maintain harmonious relations are the result of years of discipline. In other words, *wa* is the acquired characteristic of a people who have been confined for long centuries to a limited, traditional circle, and it is certainly a meritorious basis for creating national consensus.

Wa also means "circle" when it is written in a different Chinese character. This leads us to think of the early competitive peoples enclosed in a circle (the isolated lands), who were supposed to have concord by all means to prevent disruptive conflicts. Therefore, the real meaning of *wa* should be stated as "harmonious cohesion in a circle." In fact, *wa* in Japan has always meant concord among those in a group. Thus the competitiveness of the Japanese people has become invisible under the highest ethic of the nation.

Almost all books on Japan state that *wa*, as the principle of human behavior, was derived both from the Buddhist concept of benevolence and from Confucian teachings. Undoubtedly, the culture of Japan was significantly influenced by both Confucianism and Buddhism. But it is important to note that these two "isms" were later influences on the culture and that the original character of the people was "competitiveness."

It is apparent from history that Confucianism in the fifth century and Buddhism in the sixth century were introduced in Japan to meet the needs of the rulers. The administrators of the nation promulgated the Confucian tradition of obedience to superiors and the Buddhist concept of benevolence, which are ideal ethics for controlling people's emotions and preventing revolt within the community.

By the same token, Christianity would not have been excluded in the Tokugawa era (1603–1867) if the administrators had found some need for this cultural invasion. Initially Christianity did make some inroads. There was a bribery scandal involving two Japanese Christian officials of the Tokugawa Bakufu (shogun's government) and, more seriously, exposure of what seemed to be a plot by certain Japanese Christians to overthrow the Bakufu with the aid of foreign troops. A number of such events combined to make Tokugawa Ieyasu (founder of the Tokugawa Bakufu) increasingly suspicious of Christianity. In 1612 and again the following year, Ieyasu issued edicts prohibiting Christianity. But these were not strictly enforced. Another edict put forward in 1614 ordered all foreign missionaries to gather in Nagasaki and then to leave Japan for good. The Tokugawa government rooted out the faith, and after the seventeenth century Christianity, like Communism in the 1930s, was excluded from the land. In the end, the Tokugawa Bakufu decided to put an end to all further intercourse with foreigners. In addition, the Bakufu decreed that any Japanese who tried to leave the country did so under punishment of death, and that death would be awaiting any Japanese who, having left the country, tried to return. Only the Dutch and some Chinese were permitted to carry on trade with the Japanese, but they were confined to Dejima (a small island in Nagasaki Harbor) and their ships were rationed and strictly controlled.

The closing of the country in the seventeenth century had significant consequences for Japan that are apparent to this day. In the fifteenth and sixteenth centuries, Japanese traders and fishermen made their adventurous mark in various parts of Asia. There were small communities of Japanese in the Philippines, Thailand, and elsewhere. But the natural expansion of the energetic Japanese race was terminated by Tokugawa policy. Certainly the story of European colonization in Asia would have taken a very different course if the Tokugawa Bakufu had not forced the Japanese to isolate themselves from the world at the very moment when the Renaissance was in full bloom in Europe. The international influences that did reach Japan, through the Dutch at Dejima, were hardly sufficient to keep the Japanese abreast of the movement of civilization in contemporary Europe. As a result, Japan dropped far behind Europe in scientific and industrial achievements.

The Tokugawa shogunate established a complicated but effective structure of administrative control to forestall any possibility of internal revolt. It was a clever and rigid administration, in which the *daimyō* (feudal lords; more specifically, "outer" lords) were granted virtual autonomy within their territories but were watched by the Bakufu through its network of agents with close, unwearying vigilance. There is no space to state all phases of the process here. However, one of the main features was a permanent "hostage" system, in which every *daimyō* was compelled to alternate residences, spending one year in his fief and the following year in the shogunal capital of Edo. When he was in his fief, the *daimyō* had to leave his wife and family behind him in Edo. Thus any *daimyō* contemplating rebellion had to make a great effort to get his family away to safety.

To strengthen control in its own domains, the Tokugawa Bakufu prescribed for the common people, as well as for the samurai class, meticulous rules affecting most phases of their daily life, including their dwelling places, their clothing, and especially the principles governing their social intercourse. These rules became the model for the *daimyō* in the administration of their fiefs. All over Japan, they disseminated the rules of conduct and etiquette laid down by shogunal regulations. For the samurai class in particular, a strict set of disciplines was established according to Confucian teachings. The most exemplary of these was *bushidō*, or the moral code of the *bushi* (warriors, samurai). *Bushidō* means a Spartan devotion by a warrior class to the arts of battle, a readiness for self-sacrifice, and loyalty to a martial superior. Its origin can be traced back before the Tokugawa era, at least to the twelfth century. But it was during the Tokugawa period that the concept of loyalty as a vital constituent of *bushidō* achieved semireligious status. The most typical expressions of *bushidō* are found in a volume entitled *Hagakure*, popularly known as *Analects of the Nabeshima Clan*, written about the year 1716. In this samurai bible we find a famous saying: "*Bushidō to wa shinu koto to mitsuketari.*" ("*Bushidō* consists in dying" is the conclusion we have reached.) The correct interpretation of this saying is "*Bushidō* has its foundation in dedicating one's life unconditionally to one's master's service."

In short, *bushidō* was a moral code of self-sacrifice and self-effacement which in the extreme led to self-satisfaction. This clear sense of individual self-sacrifice governed the country in feudal times, because all the shoguns of the Tokugawa line, who were sincere patrons of Buddhist institutions as well, made Confucianism into the orthodox ideology of the state.

Under such rigid social constraints, an individual could have value and identity only by dissolving himself into the social group. Everybody learned to cultivate his individuality in ways that were socially acceptable and to control his emotional expression. Thus thousands of Japanese found true self-expression only through the nature-loving literature, the various forms of art, and other individual pursuits. Since the hierarchical system was rigidly regulated, a person could have individual identity only commensurate with his social status. In other words, a person's value as a citizen increased as his position got closer to the lord and decreased as it got further from the lord. Therefore, it was conceived that a human being achieved the highest virtue by serving his superior, the feudal lord, instead of regarding himself as independent from others. All the feudal virtues contained an element of self-annihilation and unselfishness. One was not to take one's own happiness or unhappiness into consideration.

Within this rigidly regimented society, no one could be self-made. Thus the competitive, adventurous Japanese of the sixteenth century became, by the nineteenth century, a docile people depending mainly on their rulers for leadership and following all orders from above with few questions. They grew accustomed to firmly established patterns of conduct, and found their ways in accordance with the traditions of their culture.

Out of this traditional background developed four cultural distinctions: (1) group-directed individualism, (2) pragmatic religion, (3) rank-consciousness, and (4) feudalistic capitalism. These are modern Japan's inheritance from the past isolation and feudalistic control. We shall now examine each one of them.

Group-Directed Individualism

Various social phenomena give evidence to the fact that "group-directed individualism" remains a cultural distinction in present-day Japanese society. This may be called a "spirit of the governed"—people preferring "mutual dependence" within a group to the autonomous exercise of individual rights and duties.

This spirit was fostered in the Japanese character during the long feudal age when people were subjected to the iron rule of the sword. It is the mother institution responsible for the passive attitude of the Japanese toward authority today.

There is a saying passed down from the Tokugawa era: "*Nagai mono niwa makarero.*" ("No matter what you say to your superiors, you have no chance of winning. So if you can't beat 'em, join 'em. Don't go against the tide.") The best policy for individuals is to go along with the direction established by the governing authorities, or to follow the consensus of the group. Yet the Japanese people find individual satisfaction in this group-directed lifestyle, owing to their belief that the prosperity of the group brings them a personal benefit to live on. This is Japan's inheritance from the Tokugawa society—the belief that the virtues of self-sacrifice and self-effacement are not necessarily incompatible with those of self-assertion and interior self-possession and that self-respect exists in the successful devotion of oneself to the group.

These traditions have enabled the Japanese people to live together in their cramped islands with relatively few outward signs of friction and violence. Nowhere in the world is governability more apparent among all classes in all situations than in Japan. In other words, few other civilized peoples are so dependent upon instructions or directions from above and on long-established rules of the group. The Japanese, if forced to rely on their own judgment away from their normal group-directed environment, will probably be more at a loss than peoples accustomed to greater individual freedom of action.

Sumo Wrestling

Sumo is the spectacular national sport of Japan, highly popular among visitors from foreign countries. Even here, in this one-on-one contest, the forces of group-directed individualism come into play.

A sumo bout gets under way with a series of ceremonial deeds. The *yobidashi kotetsu* (sumo announcer) stands in the center of the sand-made *dohyō* (ring) and calls the names of two wrestlers. One from the east side and one from the west side show up on the *dohyō*. Following an initial stamping of feet at the edge of the *dohyō*, the wrestlers pick up a handful of salt, scatter it about to purify the ring, and squat down facing each other at a respectful distance in the center of the arena. (The arena is the inner, round boundary within the square ring.) The referee keeps a watchful eye on them while barking out words of instruction.

After this ritual, the wrestlers crouch down, their noses almost touching the sand, pound the floor with their fists, and glare at each other. This set pattern, called *shikiri*, is repeated for four minutes. It is during these "four-legged" animal posturings that each wrestler seeks to read what is on the other's mind—whether his rival appears likely to spring at once to the attack or to try to ward off his opponent's onrush. Sumo starts with such psychological warfare. When time is up, the referee and the wrestlers are informed. The prebout proceedings are over. The referee crouches down, gives the word, and the contestants spring toward each other. This is the *tachi-ai* (initial clash). Then the bout begins.

The Japanese attach absolute importance to the initial clash, not only in sports but in any event of life. They believe in general that a man who is late in the initial clash usually goes down to defeat, because in their national sport, sumo, the wrestler who is up first in *tachi-ai* can usually direct the course of the bout as he pleases, putting his opponent on the defensive and often dominating him.

A sumo bout may be won either by ejecting one's opponent from the arena or by downing him inside the arena. In the former case, a wrestler goes down to defeat if so much as a toe is over the edge; in the latter case, the bout is lost if any part of the body above the feet hits the sandy dirt. The 48 recognized techniques for winning are almost impossible to translate, for a rival may be thrown, pushed, pulled, slapped, crushed, and so on, either down or out. The referee decides the winner immediately.

The bout is vigorously competitive within the narrow arena. Two gigantic bodies tackle at full capacity, hurtle through space, and fall down with a thud somewhere in the ring. It is often difficult for the referee to determine the winner. Occasionally one behemoth is thrown beautifully out of the arena while his opponent remains inside it. In such a case the winner is apparent in the eyes of spectators. However, there could be a critical moment that alters the outcome. For example, if a wrestler steps even a third of an inch outside the arena before sending his rival out of the arena, he would be the loser. The referee has to keep his eyes wide open so as not to miss these delicate points. But a referee is only human, and of course makes mistakes sometimes.

In most sports in the world, the referee or umpire is supposed to efface himself, making his decision impartially while maintaining control of the game. His decision is absolute, even if he makes a mistake as a result of the close plays. He calls them as he sees them. His judgment cannot be challenged by the players or by the fans. This is not so in sumo. Seated at intervals around the ring are five *kensayaku* (overseeing judges). Should the decision of the referee be in doubt or should he err in his judgment, a protest would come from one or more of these judges. Then follows what is known as a *mono-ii,* or appealing verdict. The five judges hoist themselves out of their seats into the ring and discuss the critical moment, using gestures to indicate what has happened. The referee, a long-trained professional, cannot participate in these deliberations. He simply awaits the outcome. The conclusion drawn by the five judges sometimes reverses the decision of the referee. This system of judgment is based on the Japanese sense of justice—the belief that the decision of victory should be fair and that any mistake should be corrected by the group. In Japan, a group's conclusion generally supersedes an individual member's decision.

Of course, despite a lot of close plays in the ring, the referee's calls are usually accurate and are not often protested by the judges. As a rule, his decisions are accepted, and he finds self-satisfaction in performing his duty without any protest from the group. This is what I have described as group-directed individualism (the inner willingness or desire of an individual to be directed by the group). Whenever individualism appears in Japanese society, it is surrounded and controlled by the group. Therefore, the basic ethical principle governing individual behavior is duty or loyalty to the group. Every public performance of an individual is directed by this principle.

Prime Minister's Individuality

As another example of group-directed individualism, I take up the case of the present Prime Minister of Japan, Zenko Suzuki. Mr. Suzuki stressed team spirit in his inaugural speech when the ruling Liberal-Democratic party chose him as its leader. He said: "I believe the most important foundation of politics is the concept of *wa* to achieve unification of varied and different abilities for attaining a higher goal." Indirectly, he insisted on integration of the party members and warned against possible factional divisiveness.

This new party leader was placed on the scene unexpectedly as a consequence of the internal conflicts of the party. The former Prime Minister, Masayoshi Ohira, was thrown out of office by the opposition parties' vote of nonconfidence, supported by the factional revolt in the ruling party. Then Masayoshi Ohira died suddenly during the general election campaign, and two capable factional heads went into desperate competition to succeed to the post of Prime Minister. The ruling party was internally divided and suffered a crisis bordering on a split. However, some political "fixers" behind the curtain created the necessary consensus and paved the way for the selection of Mr. Suzuki, who enjoyed a quiet reputation as an adroit practitioner of compromise. The split was avoided. The details of how it was done are not known to the public, but the important point is that the concord (*wa*) of the party was maintained and the fierce competition between the two factional heads was tactfully suppressed. Thus two strong individual personalities were controlled and dissolved by the group.

As a result, the new Prime Minister was expected to listen to all the voices coming out of the factional groups. Indeed, when the opposing voices of the factional leaders became too strong, even the draft of his keynote speech to the parliamentary assembly was amended by his cabinet ministers. As the head of the cabinet, a Prime Minister has to observe the general trend of the group and set aside his individuality. Otherwise, he loses control. Taking action based on the consensus of cabinet members is what gives a leader the self-assurance to qualify for his role and to ascertain his personal dignity.

Group Approach to Quality Control

The quality control of products has been outstanding in Japanese industrial plants and has been considered the key factor in Japan's successful expansion of exports. Of course, this production technique did not originate in Japan but was imported from the United States. In assimilating the imported technique, Japanese management added a unique group-directed approach to it. They put a T in front of the QC and made it "total quality control." TQC encompasses the activities of the entire company and its members, extending even to the workers' emotions, and it directs the way that every group of workers plunges spiritedly into the job.

Japanese workers have been imbued with clear objectives of quality control and a sense that high-quality production is important to them, to their union, to their families, and to their country. Workers and management thus share the same objectives. Each plant has its white-collar and blue-collar quality control circles, in which three to ten employees meet on their own time and analyze work standards and ways to improve the product. Each QC circle works like a group of brothers and competes with every other group for gaining pride of workmanship.

The cultural traits of mutual help and competitiveness have fortified the system and fueled workers' enthusiasm. Individual idleness cannot be tolerated within the group. It is a competition of allegiance in which the rewards for applicable ideas are mostly psychological. In contrast to the employee suggestion programs in the USA, which often offer workers up to $10,000 for useful innovations, in Japan an award of $1,000 for a patentable idea is considered generous. Companywide credit goes to the group that makes the most valuable improvement and thus raises a competitive fever in the factory. Every group is challenged to capture the prize, and accordingly workmanship rises at the plant.

Educational as well as cultural factors have contributed to the success of quality production in Japan. It is well known that the Japanese educational system is extremely uniform in nature, producing good industrial forces at the prevailing level. The human resources for industry produced by the Japanese and American educational systems may be compared roughly as in Figure 2.

The Japanese educational system, with its highly uniform manner of teaching, produces fewer dropouts than the American system and at the same time fewer geniuses who are able to invent new technologies. But it produces many more standardized or average workers who are able to accomplish the routine jobs perfectly and who can learn to improve their skills. On the other hand, to my understanding, the flexible and developmental American system of teaching produces a lot of geniuses who rebel against being forced to conform but at the same time produces more dropouts (reportedly as high as 3 percent of the population) who are substandard as industrial forces. When one

Figure 2. Human resources produced by education in the
United States and Japan.

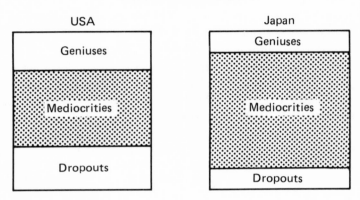

of these dropouts comes into the production lines of a plant, the quality of an end product is bound to suffer. With today's production process, which is divided into many interlocking steps, one substandard worker could spoil the whole production line. In terms of quality production, then, Japan is apparently at an advantage. Its major problem is improving its educational system to increase the number of geniuses, whereas America has the acute problem of reducing the number of dropouts.

In summary, total quality control has been deployed like a newly emerged religion in Japan, because the people are monolithic and easily fall into a feverish enthusiasm when it comes to maintaining the pride of their group. On this note, let us take a look at the religious background of the Japanese people.

Pragmatic Religion

Religion is a part of every society. It is a cultural product of mankind, a tool for survival. The often heard comment "The Japanese don't have any religion" is the most superficial of observations. It is true that in the eyes of foreigners the Japanese would seem to lack firm religious belief. A couple married at a Shinto shrine may have both a Shinto and a Buddhist altar in their home, and may also be members of a Bible study group in which they sing hymns praising Jesus Christ. When they die, they will choose Buddhist burial rites. Such behavior is often considered extremely odd by non-Japanese.

But in fact the Japanese are rich in religious feeling. What is Japanese religion, then? In a word, ancestor worship. In ancient times, the Japanese social structure was strictly controlled and regulated by the patriarch of *ie* (family or clan). The patriarch was responsible to the higher authorities of the nation as well as to his ancestors for his behavior. At the top of the nation, the Emperor himself was responsible to his ancestors for his behavior.

In this patriarchical value system, there could be no room for the concept of an "Almighty God," as in the traditions of Judaism, Christianity, and Islam. On the contrary, Japanese *kami* (gods) are not considered separate personalities from men. In need of salvation and help, people turn to the superiors of *ie* (that is, their ancestors), who are believed to be gods. Another traditional belief in Japan is that the dead go to the place of their ancestors and become *kami*. This heavy emphasis on ancestor worship is the basis of Japanese religious feeling and was a powerful impulse among the people in the isolated village communities in ancient times. The contemporary Japanese are no exception.

In discussing the history of Japanese religions, I must limit myself to pointing out a few main historical developments, since there is no room in a book such as this to cover the subject thoroughly.

Shinto

Strictly speaking, Japan has three main religious traditions: Shinto, Buddhism, and Christianity. It is thought that Shinto developed from the belief systems of the tribes that inhabited the rice-planting areas of the Japanese archipelago. Primitive Shinto began in the form of *ujigami,* a tutelary or guardian shrine system in which each family or clan (*uji* means a surname) had its own shrine as a central symbol of its dedication to the "ancestral spirit." The spirits of ancestors were thus worshiped and enshrined by each successive generation of descendants, and after many years people made a religion of their worshiping. A remnant of this religion of ancestor worship can still be seen in the unique village festivals of rural Japan.

Maintaining its hereditary good name and continuing its ancestors' glorious work was the most important responsibility of a family. The religion also set up certain ethical standards for family members. However, no provision was made for the salvation of the individual; instead, the ultimate destiny of an individual was to lose his identity and merge with his ancestral spirits after death.

Anyone familiar with the history and mythology of Japan will agree that Japan's beginnings can be traced to a time when one clan triumphed over the other clans and made them subservient to its rule. It is quite conceivable that the conquering clan united the various clan gods together under the banner of its own deity. Political considerations were of course part of this consolidation, but it was assisted by the homogeneous nature of the Japanese people. When Amaterasu Omikami, the Sun Goddess, was given centrality by the most victorious clan, all Japanese became a people under her protective reign. Thus a nationwide religion, Shinto, was born. It emerged from the primeval worship of clan gods. Shinto means "the way of the gods," an idea borrowed from the old Chinese concept "mandate of heaven."

When the Ainu people living in northern and eastern Japan were defeated by the Genji clan, they were made kin and admitted to the family with the surname Abe. If we investigate the origins of Japanese families named Abe today, we will find that almost all of them derived from the Genji clan. And it is said that if we follow any Japanese family far enough back into history, it will be traceable to one of four clans: Minamoto (Genji), Taira, Fujiwara, or Tachibana. Since all four of these clans regard the Emperor as their founder, all Japanese are, theoretically speaking, one large family.

The militarism that came on stage following the great Meiji Restoration (1868) forced all Japanese to worship the Emperor as a central figure and Amaterasu Omikami as the ancestor of the Japanese Imperial Family. Thus "State Shinto" was established—a political and religious system which stressed the divinity of the Emperor. But this attempt could not have succeeded if it had not been supported by two beliefs already entrenched strongly among the Japanese—namely, the belief that everyone on the island originally descended from the Imperial Family line and the strong belief in *ujigami* (clan gods).

However, you might not get many yeses from the Japanese to the question "Do you believe in Shinto?" The spirit of Shinto is communicated in myriad ways—in the Japanese architecture made of cypress wood, in the tea ceremony, in flower arrangement, and in the New Year's celebration. The fine spirit of Shinto flows silently through the hearts of the Japanese. The essence of Japanese life is found in this unconscious, unapprehended tradition. One reason the Japanese themselves are unaware of it is because of Shinto's pantheistic nature. "Eight million gods" are recognized. Every clan created many of its own distinct objects of worship, so depending upon the sect, we find different gods. These clan gods have colored Japanese life to a considerable degree.

Since a farming people's life cycle reaches completion every year and renews itself, as it were, each spring, the Japanese have come to appreciate the changing seasons greatly and to find a concept of eternity in them. The many festivals held at different times throughout the four seasons express gratitude to the ancestors. In many rural areas of Japan people have a custom of climbing a hill after the rice planting or harvest to offer thanks to the gods enshrined on the hill. Depending on the local tradition, there may be phallic or sexual objects worshiped at the shrines. These are the male and female forms of gods, made of stone, wood, or other materials. The ancient Japanese explained the birth of Japan as the result of the mating of the gods, which demonstrates the religious power they sensed in sexual union. The sexual act, duplicating the divine activity, is a means not only of communicating with the gods (the ancestors) but also of producing descendants, which is considered a holy act. Thus the worship of sexual organs is in a sense the worship of creativity and shows the Japanese appreciation of their ancestors.

Buddhism

Buddhism entered Japan in the sixth century by way of Kudara on the Korean peninsula. The teachings of Buddha originated in India, spread to China, and were finally brought to Japan. After the Japanese ingested the teachings, they transformed them tremendously to suit their character. The major transformation was an emphasis on worshiping the spirits of the dead, a departure from the strict precepts of Buddhism. Of course, the doctrines of Buddhism were also respected, but the most influential ideas the Japanese gleaned from Buddhist scriptures were that our present life on earth is only temporary, that the real life is in the world to come, and that after death there is a heaven or a hell.

The most common Buddhist practice in Japan, therefore, has been praying for rebirth in paradise. People who are approaching death begin to devote their minds to spiritual matters, chanting, *"Namu-amida-butsu"* or *"Namu-myoho-renge-kyo"* ("May my soul rest in peace, merciful Buddha"). They embrace religious faith as they near death because they regard religion as a means of passing from this world to the next. If they act with

the utmost sincerity of heart, they are sure to attain final enlightenment, for Buddha, as the object of faith and the possessor of
infinite love, will take everyone unto him. This is a popularized
interpretation of Buddhism in Japan.

All these religious phenomena reveal the Japanese devotion
to their ancestors. The relics of ancestors are enshrined in the
Buddhist altar of the home. Those who die are interred in the
same grave with their ancestors, and their happiness in the
afterlife is prayed for. At the two *higan* (going to the other shore)
festivals in spring and autumn, families crowd the graveyards to
pay their respects to their ancestors. Few other peoples place
such importance on visiting graves as do the Japanese. On
special anniversary days decorative altars are erected, votive
lights are lit, and a Buddhist monk from a nearby temple is
invited to recite the scriptures before the family altar. When
something important is accomplished or a joyful event occurs,
the Japanese say, "I must bow before the grave and show my
gratitude," or "I must report to the ancestors." It seems that a
majority of the Japanese have combined their ancestors, the gods
of Shinto, and the Buddhist deities into one beneficent image of
God and feel that they are watched over and protected by that
image.

For this reason, many a family has both a Shinto and a
Buddhist altar in the house with no feeling of contradiction. The
dead are thought to reside in the relics placed in these altars. The
remains of the dead are sacred objects in Japan. After World War
II many Japanese returned to the site of some wartime battles to
retrieve the remains of a relative or a friend who died there.
Though this might strike the Westerner as odd, it is an indication
of the depth of the Japanese religious spirit.

In Japan, Buddhism was transformed into a religion that
worships departed souls, follows the teachings of the ancestors,
and prays for their blessings. This is "ancestor worship," pure
and simple. Japanese ancestor worship emphasizes communica-

tion between the living and the dead. It is a unique religious phenomenon.

Christianity

Islam spread as far as Southeast Asia, but failed to reach Japan. However, Christianity penetrated the islands in the early sixteenth century and gathered ardent Japanese followers. The reason for the successful invasion may be that Christianity views the dead person as someone who has been called to his master in Heaven—a concept not unlike the relationship with one's ancestors in traditional Japanese religion. According to a recent survey, the number of registered Christians in Japan is a little over 970,000—less than 1 percent of the total population. But close to 1.4 million Bibles are sold every year, and about 9 million copies of partial editions of the Gospels of Mark and Luke are sold. In grand total, the number surpasses 10 million copies. In other words, one in every ten people in Japan buys a Bible every year.

The medieval rulers Oda Nobunaga and Toyotomi Hideyoshi (conquerors in the Turbulent Age, before the Tokugawa period) allowed Christianity into Japan because they wanted the culture package of which the religion was part and parcel—quite a different motive from the one that pertained to Buddhism's introduction. (Buddhism was introduced into Japan in the sixth century because the rulers believed its concept of benevolence would prevent revolt from the people.) When Christianity entered Rome, it drove out all the Roman deities. When it entered Germany, it destroyed the native gods and took control of people's hearts. In the same way, when Christianity entered Japan, it inspired an anti-Buddhist movement among Christian converts. Christians in Kyushu (the large southern island of Japan) destroyed most of the ancient Buddhist statues and temples there. Eventually even Nobunaga, who was fond of novelties, recognized the danger that Christianity posed to Japan. The extreme exclusivity of the Christian religion ran counter to the Japanese eclectic spirit, which is willing to accept many different things at the same time. As a result, Christianity became the object of persecution in a way no other religion ever has been in Japan, and was completely shut out of the country through the long Tokugawa period.

Though Christianity was welcomed when it came in, as Confucianism and Buddhism had been before it, its ultimate refusal to recognize ancestor worship resulted in its rejection. When St. Francis Xavier, a Portuguese Jesuit missionary, came to Japan in 1549 to promulgate Christianity, he was extremely dismayed by the strong ancestor worship of the Japanese. The people accepted his teachings but hesitated to turn themselves to Christianity because their ancestors died in the spirit of other religions and they would not be able to face those ancestors in the afterworld if they became Christians. After World War II, Christianity swept into Korea and other areas that had been devastated by the war and as a result of active proselytizing gained many converts. But it was not able to reestablish a foothold in Japan, the most ravaged of all nations. Again, its strong exclusivity seems to have been the cause.

A brief outline of the history of Christianity in Japan is presented below.

History of Christianity in Japan

1549   St. Francis Xavier lands in Kagoshima in southwestern Japan (Aug. 15). This is the first contact between the Roman Catholic Church and Japan. Xavier reportedly decided to engage in missionary work in Japan after meeting a Japanese named Yajiro in Malacca in 1547.

1550   Xavier and Brother Fernandez travel to Kyoto, Japan's capital at the time, to try to obtain an audience with the Emperor. Their hope is not fulfilled, but some 100 Japanese turn Christian during Xavier's stay in Japan between 1550 and 1551.

1560 Father Gaspar Vilela meets Shogun Ashikaga Yoshiteru and receives an official permit to preach Christianity in Japan. Local leaders who convert to Christianity in or after 1561 include Omura Sumitada, Takayama Ukon, and Otomo Sorin.

1569 The first Christian church is opened in Nagasaki.

1585 A Japanese youth delegation is received in audience by Pope Gregory XIII in Rome. The number of Christians in Japan reportedly reaches 100,000.

1587 Shogun Toyotomi Hideyoshi suddenly orders the banishment of missionaries—the beginning of more than two and a half centuries of persecution of Christians by Japanese leaders. Hideyoshi also orders the exile of Takayama Ukon, a spiritual leader of Japanese Christians.

1597 Twenty-six Christians are martyred in Nagasaki (Feb. 5).

1614 Shogun Tokugawa Ieyasu, Hideyoshi's successor, issues an order prohibiting Christianity in Japan and adopts the *efumi* system, in which people are forced to step on the cross, on pictures of Christ and the Virgin Mary, and on other Christian symbols to demonstrate to the Tokugawa Bakufu that they are not believers.

1622 Fifty-five Christians are killed in Nagasaki.

1637 Some 10,000 farmers, mostly Christians, stage the Shimabara Rebellion against the local government. The Tokugawa government puts down the rebellion a year later and strengthens its policy of isolating Japan from foreign influences.

1858 *Efumi* is abolished.

1865 The Oura (Christian) Church is built in Nagasaki, available to foreigners only.

1873 The government order prohibiting Christianity is abolished, 286 years after Hideyoshi banned the religion.

1885   Pope Leo XII sends a letter to Emperor Meiji through Bishop Osouf.

1889   Freedom of religion is granted by the Meiji Constitution (Feb. 11).

"Once you believe, you can find religion even in the head of a sardine" goes a colorful Japanese saying, which means that God is to be found anywhere in the hearts of people. The Japanese were polytheists from the start and have the unique spiritual ability to make almost anything an object of worship. They are culturally omnivorous, able to consume and digest all sorts of things—and with little upset to the stomach. They manage to choose what will suit their needs and absorb it ingeniously into their culture. This is the Japanese "cultural stomach" and its workings.

There is a large graveyard known as the Kamakura Cemetery near my home. It is a Buddhist-style cemetery, built by a Japanese company, but there is absolutely no religious discrimination against its "residents." A glance at the gravestones, the shapes of the graves, and the posthumous names written on the tablets kept at the graves reveals at once that Jodo-shu Buddhists, Zen-shu Buddhists, and Nichiren-shu Buddhists are buried there. One of the graves has the strikingly nonreligious shape of a rugby ball. There are even a few graves with crucifixes on them, and they stand out. This is a truly Japanese scene, with people of many different religious faiths buried together in the same area.

Flexibility is a trait that characterizes the Japanese in all their encounters with other cultures. When the Japanese take something in, they redirect or assimilate it to suit their preferences. Even Christianity seems to be treading this path in Japan. The fundamental tenet of Christianity is "God loves us"—but how long will it be before this precept receives the cultural overlay and becomes "Our ancestors love us" in Japan? Though it is still a matter of speculation, the "Japanese stomach" may well digest Christianity the way it did Buddhism.

Uchimura Kanzo, a famous Japanese Christian, once talked of his love for the two J's. One of these J's was Jesus and the other was Japan. Let us hear what he said: "Jesus and Japan. My belief doesn't have one central circle as a core. It is made up of two half-circles. These two strengthen each other; Jesus strengthens my love for Japan, and purifies it. Japan assures my love for Jesus, and provides a strong base for me to love Jesus." In other words, his religious belief and his patriotism are tied together and reinforce each other. Patriotism is love of the country handed down to us by our forefathers; accordingly, it includes love directed toward our ancestors. This beautiful double structure makes up the belief of Mr. Uchimura.

More than a few Japanese industrialists have successfully combined religious faith and love for their company. Many companies consciously model their policy or motto after the Buddhist or Christian spirit. One manufacturer of precision measuring instruments has incorporated the Buddhist ideal of *wa* (harmony) into its policy and is using it to put a very special kind of management into practice. Every month, workers attend a special Ancestor Ceremony. The liturgy of this service proceeds from unison singing of the company song, to an offering of flowers and votive lights, to a chant of praise to the Buddha. It is followed by a complete Buddhist service with offerings of incense, *nembutsu* (an invocation), a sermon, and hymns for the deceased parents of company employees. The ceremony is carried out at every plant of the company and is attended by workers who have no connection with Jodo-shu Buddhism—by Christians and by other non-Buddhists who work for the company.

Thus the Ancestor Ceremony appeals to a common feeling. It is interesting to note that this ceremony, translated into the appropriate languages, is also held at the company's overseas branches in America, West Germany, and Singapore, and at its factories in Brazil. Even non-Japanese are willing to join in the

Buddhist-style service. Apparently, the idea of "honoring the ancestors" is quite inoffensive, and in the form of a musical liturgy it is an enjoyable event even for Christians or non-Japanese employees. So factory workers in Brazil are singing Buddhist hymns in Portuguese!

The Japanese have such a pliant and multifaceted religious consciousness that, to the outside observer, they may indeed appear to be without religious faith. However, the Japanese people have a unique ability to embrace and absorb a wide variety of religious systems. Just as the Shinto gods and the buddhas of India and China were dissolved into the congregation of ancient Japanese ancestors, so Christianity may end up as a part of Japanese polytheism. The Japanese can worship two gods at the same time without any feeling of contradiction.

On January 1, 1981, I received hundreds of New Year's greeting cards, as many a Japanese did. (Approximately 2.9 million greeting cards were mailed celebrating that New Year's Day.) One of them was from an ardent Christian. (See Figure 3.)

At the top of the card is written the traditional celebrating word "Gashun"—"Gratitude for Spring." This phrase for the New Year is quite common in Japan. But looking closely at it, we find that it is based on the lunar calendar (in which the New Year begins in early spring) and has a little flavor of Shintoism. Below that phrase, the writer has added an excerpt from the Gospel of St. John, Chapter 6: "Lord, to whom shall we go? You have the words of eternal life." Below the Gospel, she expresses her political opinion for the year: "The voice for the revision of the constitution—to its detriment—is becoming larger. However, we should discuss not only Article 9 but also the Emperor system." This statement sounds as if the writer were opposed to the Emperor system.* She can say anything, of course, under the

---

*In contrast to the ambiguous role of the Emperor under the old constitution, in which all power was believed to stem from him and his divinity was supported by the whole cult of "State Shinto," the postwar constitution of 1947 defined the Emperor as "the symbol of the state and of the unity of the people." Thus "State Shinto" was abolished, and the present Emperor system is a symbolic one.

Figure 3. Japanese New Year's greeting.

賀 春
1981年 元旦

主よ、われら誰にゆかん、永遠の生命の
言葉は汝にあり(新約ヨハネ伝6章)

　新しい年を迎えご一家の上に新しい希望が充ちあふれ
ますように。憲法改悪右傾化の声が騒がしくなりつつ
ありますが9条のみならず、天皇制も大いに論議すべき
です。忘れてならないことは36年前の敗戦の日の原点に
立って、日本が世界平和の礎となることでしょう。かつ、生
きとし生けるものの生命が尊重される社会になるよう祈り
斗いましょう。

right of free speech, but in Japan negative comments about the
Emperor system usually come from the left.

　One may be puzzled to note that the card includes three
features: Shintoism, Christianity, and a seemingly pro-
communist attitude. Very few Japanese themselves are aware of
such a mixture in their daily life. Yet the phenomenon is not
unusual in Japan.

　In summary, the Japanese have created a double structure
in their religious life and possess a great deal of flexibility that
permits them to move back and forth between the poles. This is
why I have titled the section "Pragmatic Religion."

The Rank-Conscious Society

The Tokugawa period was the age of politics. Under Tokugawa rule, political unity and control were effected for the first time in Japanese history, and a rigid social order was devised to regulate the people. During 260 years of undisturbed peace, unparalleled in world history, the Tokugawa samurai developed a bureaucracy and gained increased administrative capability, for they had to rule the fiefs and the feudal citizens in peace. Thus they were no longer warriors but rather bureaucrats of a kind. The center of the samurai bureaucracy was in Edo (Osaka prospered as the center of merchant activities). To strengthen its feudalistic control, the Tokugawa Bakufu enforced a rigid hierarchy of *shi-nō-kō-shō:* the samurai *(shi)* at the top, followed by the peasants *(nō)*, the craftsmen *(kō)*, and the merchants *(shō)* at the bottom. The peasants were ranked second because the samurai believed that agriculture was the only true source of wealth and measured their salaries in bushels of rice. The merchants were ranked at the bottom because they were considered to produce nothing but to gain huge profits simply by trading the products of others. The boast of the samurai was that they were indifferent to money, the symbol of materialism. They looked down on the merchants.

The term "samurai" actually stands for a complicated hierarchy with shogun at the top, followed by *daimyō* (feudal lords) and their subordinates (ordinary samurai). From shogun to *ashigaru* (the bottom rank of samurai), there were approximately 20 hierarchical ranks. Even at the *daimyō* level there was an upper class and a lower class. The same was true of peasants, craftsmen, and merchants; many different status levels divided them into hierarchical strata. Within any given hierarchy, people were further classified by age. The feudalistic administration even set up a class below the merchant stratum—the lowest group, called the "outcast." It has long since vanished in Japan.

All these hierarchical orders in Japanese society were maintained in hereditary fashion until the Meiji Restoration (1868). It was natural for a Japanese to adjust his interpersonal relations in accordance with the various levels of hierarchy he encountered. Honorific words developed in abundance because everyone had to deal cautiously with superiors and cut his way through the rank-conscious jungle. Whenever two people met in the course of daily events, they had to decide on the spur of the moment who was superior and who was inferior. The superior could puff himself up and make much of his position while the inferior was expected to crouch down in humility and subservience. This art of adjusting the self in response to a social superior or inferior was important in the Tokugawa period. The best defensive skill of the inferior was to "hold the tongue." But in order to communicate his will or intention he had to express himself somehow, so he spoke in vague words. Even for the superior, the ideal communications technique in this rank-conscious society was indirection, or euphemistic language.

The extreme form of this technique was the noteworthy *haragei* (literally, "art of belly"), meaning "communication by intuitiveness." In this ingenious method of communication, a person just smiled at others and flattered them with his inexpressible charm, all the while hemming and hawing and never committing himself to a clear statement of his ambition or plan. *Haragei*—letting the partner probe, or intuitively uncovering his real intention—was certainly a highly advanced form of communication for this feudalistic, rank-conscious society.

A few years after the Tokugawa Bakufu collapsed, the Meiji government legally wiped out the strong class distinctions. This sharp break with the feudal hierarchical system was an amazing achievement for the Meiji administration. Eventually the samurai category was dropped entirely. Today, some families may occasionally make reference to their distinguished roots but not so much as the supposed descendants of *The Mayflower* or the nobilities in England do. Young Japanese are apparently not as interested as young Englishmen in such matters as the blood in their veins.

However, the culture rooted during the Tokugawa period still pervades Japanese society, giving it its nature and character. The rank-consciousness of the society has also made the language elusive. The Japanese language rarely conveys its meaning with clarity, or rather, the Japanese rarely state their meaning clearly. They are always halting or hesitating. Blunt statements very often invite hostility or rejection. People are expected to state the minimum amount in a reserved manner, as if they were afraid to commit themselves one way or the other. In Japanese the verb is placed at the end of the sentence, with the affirmative or negative particle coming at the end of the verb. Thus a speaker can easily break off halfway through a sentence without committing himself. The Japanese people are traditionally reluctant to give a clear yes or no answer, especially when they have to make a decision with little time to think. When forced to make a statement in such absolute terms, many a Japanese will naturally hedge.

Foreigners are often annoyed by this cultural trait, but some of them subsequently come to admire it. They realize that it contains a practical human wisdom, an application of the wise old proverb "Look before you leap." The Japanese don't avoid yes and no in ordinary conversation as a matter of principle. They just try to anticipate the result before saying yes or no. Since human relationships are a key factor in this emotional society, the Japanese prefer not to influence others' feelings one way or the other by saying yes as a sign of like or no with a nuance of dislike. Their cultural tradition binds them to withhold free expression of their likes and dislikes. This tradition also affects the relationship between husband and wife, as we will see in Chapter 3.

Today in Japan class distinctions, both formal and informal, are extremely weak. The Japanese have created a very egalitarian society, enjoying the fruits of economic development.

In fact, Japan's unique brand of group-centeredness and group affiliation works against any class feeling. Japanese society is divided into numerous groups, each composed of many status layers. That is, the typical Japanese group is made up, not of people of the same status and function, but of people of different functions and status. This is what Chie Nakane means by a "vertical society" in her book *Japanese Society*. In contrast, American society has a more horizontal structure, with groups made up primarily of peers. In Japan, intergroup associations are weak and hierarchical relationships within each group are always vertical. Naturally, the Japanese don't identify themselves in class terms, and when asked to do so, about 90 percent opt for the middle class; this has been disclosed by frequent questionnaire surveys. Formal class distinctions have all but disappeared in Japan.

Nevertheless, Tokugawa-style rank-consciousness, though it may have relaxed a little, remains, and the skill of adjusting the "self" is still crucial for human relations in Japanese society today. It is enlightening to talk with an owner of any little restaurant frequented by business executives. His remarks will always be the same: "When members of Company X show up for a drink, I can tell without fail who is the most important, who's next, who comes after that, and on down the line." First of all, he can tell from their manner of speech. Even if there is only one year's difference in length of service between two employees, the elder will address the younger by *kun,* and the younger will address the elder by *san* (suffixes to their names). This is the skill of adjusting the "self" in response to a partner.

The Japanese company has a pyramidal structure, with people linked in vertical relationships. No matter what special skills or abilities a person has, he will not be regarded as important by society at large unless he has a title, especially the title of *chō* (chief). As a result, everyone aims for administrative work, where such titles are available in abundance.

The single Chinese character *chō* on one's *meishi* (calling card) or desk nameplate is the most important sign of status and a source of endless personal gratification for the Japanese employee. It is the reward for years and years of work under tension and stress. It is also the necessary requirement for the self-esteem of the Japanese organization man. The main significance of the exchange of *meishi* among Japanese is that it makes clear a man's rank in his organization and group affiliation—Managing Director of A Bank, Director of B Bureau, Professor of Economics at C University, and so forth. As an indication of status in the larger society, the title *kachō* (section chief) or *buchō* (department head) is much more effective than the name of one's profession, such as editor or engineer. Almost all bank salesmen and stockbrokers have the title "deputy chief" or "*kachō's* representative" on their calling cards. This is a social necessity for dealing with prospective customers and gaining their confidence.

Thus a person's title in Japan not only describes the work he does but places him in a larger social ranking that extends beyond the boundaries of his company. Many a Japanese has witnessed a complete change in attitude and manner of address after a client or associate has glanced at the calling card just passed to him. The Japanese still retain the Tokugawa-style rank-consciousness, puffing themselves up if they have a higher social position and humbling themselves if they have a lower position than their associates.

Further, a man's title also defines his wife's role in life and her social position. In the company apartment houses, for example, the rankings of husbands determine the attitudes, manners, social habits, and language of the wives. Particularly overseas, the titles of husbands seem to have extraordinary importance for

Japanese wives. When a woman arrives in the country where her husband is stationed, the first thing she will probably do is visit a neighboring Japanese woman to inquire about schools for the children and places to shop for food. In return, the first thing she is usually asked is not, for example, the ages of her children, but her husband's job status—his place of employment and his position there. A Japanese woman living abroad is always identified and addressed not by her own name, but by her husband's company's name and job title—for instance, "Oku-san (wife) of X-san at the Japan Bank," or "Oku-san of the Branch Head." Women with higher-ranking husbands become friends, and those with lower-ranking husbands form their own group. Even at parties, the seating is arranged in accordance with the husbands' social rank. The order in which the wives speak, the amount of their contribution to the conversation, and their manner of speaking parallel their husbands' ranks and titles. Thus in Japanese society a woman gains recognition, self-esteem, and security only by virtue of the title her husband holds. The higher the status of the title, the greater the recognition and security accorded. Those who reach a suitably high status are always addressed in polite speech, but they are not required to reply in kind. This is the rank-conscious society.

Feudalistic Capitalism

It was the Tokugawa's first shogun, Ieyase, who created a centralized feudal system that seems almost the antithesis of the decentralized feudalism that once existed in Europe.

As the national economy developed during the Tokugawa period, villagers around the *daimyō*'s castle in each fief, or in the more developed parts of rural Japan, shifted their energies from subsistence farming to the processing of foodstuffs, silk, and other agricultural products. In the late eighteenth century, there was a remarkable outburst of entrepreneurial activity in rural Japan. During this period, the Tokugawa promoted the teaching of Confucian philosophy and historical studies, so that virtually the entire samurai class became literate. For that matter, most merchants and the richer peasants and craftsmen also became literate and developed themselves in mathematics. The abacus was widely used in merchant activities, and the younger generation was trained intensively on this calculating instrument in temple schools. This practice may well have contributed to the development of the strong mathematical ability of the Japanese.

The rapid growth of intellectual activities in the Tokugawa period was greatly enhanced by the intellectual cross-fertilization that resulted from the hostage system, which required the *daimyō* to alternate residences between their fiefs and their families in Edo. With the *daimyō* came a large flow of teachers and students with scholarly materials between Edo and the various domains. Just as Japan had developed into a single economic unit, so the country became a unified intellectual nation in a way unprecedented in Asia.

The Tokugawa feudal system remained strong through the first half of the nineteenth century. However, its strongest wall of defense—isolation—was threatened by the European maritime powers, which had subjugated India, taken over much of Southeast Asia, and penetrated the important coastal ports of China. In addition, the Russians had extended their hold over all of Siberia and were ambitiously pushing southward into the islands north of Japan. American ships frequented Japanese coastal waters in search of whales. All in all, in 1853 and the following years, these various Western powers compelled Japan to open its doors.

Finally, in 1858, the Tokugawa authorities lost their stand on isolation and Japan was fully opened. The administration was shaken to its foundations, and the whole feudal structure, which controlled all the *daimyō* so effectively, began to disintegrate. Some of the greater *daimyō*, especially the Choshu clan, turned against the Bakufu and openly defied the Tokugawa authority. Thus the weakened Bakufu rapidly lost control over the "outer" lords. Then a coalition of Satsuma, Choshu, and other "outer" *daimyō* seized the order of the Imperial Court, which had held only a nominal sovereign position for some centuries. In the name of the Emperor, the coalition troops—the so-called Imperial Army—announced the restoration of direct Imperial rule on January 3, 1868. Eventually, the troops also seized Edo Castle, putting an end to more than two and a half centuries of Tokugawa feudalistic rule.

The new government was led by Imperial princes, court nobles, and feudal lords (former *daimyō*), but the actual execution of policies fell largely to a group of able reformers from the Satsuma and Choshu clans.

With the old feudal domains replaced by new prefectures, Japan was remodeled and administered by officials appointed by the central government. The samurai were deprived of all their special privileges, and Japan embarked on a great social reformation. Education and personal achievements became important factors for gaining social status, and great efforts were made to modernize the economy. During this period, government bureaus and other functional organizations were established. Needless to say, a functional organization is a social unit designed to achieve certain objectives effectively. It is quite different from the village-type community and can integrate human efforts to achieve its goal.

Unfortunately or fortunately, Japan leaped into the modern era without experiencing capitalism, socialism, or industrial revolution. The explosive Meiji civilization whipped the Japanese to a gallop on the track of Westernization. Nevertheless, the Western influence could not eradicate the traditional base of feudalism in such a hurried transition period. On the contrary, the visiting culture was incorporated into the feudalistic framework of the Tokugawa era. Thus the traditional culture remained within the modernized Meiji systems. The coexistence of modernity and feudalism had begun.

What a contrast this is to the West, where feudalism was destroyed when capitalism was introduced! This is why a Japanese govenment bureau or business company today has a double character: it is both a modernized functional system and a feudalistic community. In other words, every Japanese organization contains the characteristics of what the Germans call Gesellschaft and Gemeinschaft.

Despite the flood of Western ideologies, there was little chance for Western individualism to bud and grow in the Meiji era. The reason was quite simple. Japan had to rise to a national consensus if it was to catch up with the West. When the nation opened its doors, the Japanese found themselves surrounded by Asian countries that had already fallen prey to Western colonialism. The people knew they were vulnerable to the Western invasion and could easily be swallowed by it. Thus the whole nation bound together to protect itself. There was no room for selfish behavior or individualistic action. The slogan "Rich nation, strong army" was adopted as the basis for national consensus, and politics and economics were welded together. With a social structure composed of both modern and old-fashioned elements, Japan began to construct a national economy.

On April 27, 1891, seven Russian ships entered Port Nagasaki in Kyushu Island and passed through the inland sea to Port Kobe, where they anchored. It was a show of force against Japan. Two months later, the Chinese fleet came into the Bay of Tokyo (Tokyo was the new name for Edo) and stunned the long-isolated Japanese nation with the roar of its salute guns. At the time, Japan had only a small army and a few wooden battleships. However three years later, when the Sino-Japanese War broke out, Japan had a fleet of 55 steel ships (61,300 tons in total) and defeated the Chinese fleet in the Yellow Sea. The one-sided victory was recorded.

Ten years later, in 1904, the Japanese navy under the command of Admiral Heihachiro Togo, with 152 ships (265,000 tons in total), won a resounding victory over the Russian Baltic fleet in the Japan Sea. The world was astonished at the tremendous growth of Japan's economic and militaristic powers. Even the growth of the Japanese automobile industry, which produced the first car in 1936 and made successful inroads into the American and European markets in the late 1970s, is less spectacular by comparison. These achievements were the result of Japan's ability to establish a single national consensus and to assimilate capitalism into the feudalistic society. It should be emphasized again that the basic cultural trait of the Japanese is "competitiveness." Consensus is simply a tool for channeling competitiveness toward a single national goal.

Japan Incorporated

As stated above, Japan was an economic latecomer. In the early Meiji era it was underdeveloped and, more seriously, had almost no natural resources. The people were aware that social stability and progress depended on the development of a national economy. They also recognized that the combined efforts of government and business enterprises were necessary to realize the industrialization that Japan needed to respond quickly and successfully to the challenge of the superior Western powers.

Thus the close cooperation between government and business began. This was the origin of "Japan Incorporated." The coalition was absolutely necessary to make major business investments and create a dynamic modern state. Some people think of "Japan Incorporated" as a recent phenomenon, a setup created after World War II between big business and government, as symbolized today by the Ministry of International Trade and Industry. But this is not correct. It originated in the early days of the Meiji era.

The old feudalistic order proved to be a wonderful nursery for the Meiji bureaucracy to grow. "Selfless devotion to the group," which had been the moral code of the feudal society—the esprit de corps of the Japanese—became the impetus for the efficient growth of bureaucracy and the diligent efforts of workers in the modernized Meiji organizations. Efficiency and diligence in turn accelerated the industrialization process.

The whole nation ran as an extended bureaucratic family. It was a conforming, communal-minded culture with an authoritarian hierarchy. The Meiji government took the initiative to invest in big business ventures because it could not wait for the growth of small businesses and cottage industries across Japan. This is another distinctive contrast with modern Europe, where industrial development was achieved through the growth and expansion of small-scale industries. Textiles and ammunitions were among the first projects of the Meiji government; later, shipbuilding and other heavy industries were introduced, promoted, and protected. However, the government realized that its attempt at rapid economic development, running so many projects by its own hands, was overburdening and decided to pass the projects on to private entrepreneurs. Mitsui, Mitsubishi, and other *zaibatsu* (giant business combines) rose rapidly as conglomerate business empires. Their successes were mainly attributable to their political connections with the government.

When the *zaibatsu* were dissolved after World War II, the politicians slowly but surely renewed their link with big business to reconstruct the national economy. The bureaucrats, as the nation's rigid backbone, were entrusted with reconstruction and further development. It was their task to defend and promote the national economy. On the other hand, it was essential for business companies to have good relations with the govenment in order to secure protection, promotion, and even financing. In the postwar days these contacts established a close relationship between the government and the business circle. Thus a nexus similar to the one in the Meiji era was created with even greater solidity and effectiveness and was openly dubbed "Japan Incorporated."

Today the Ministry of International Trade and Industry (the notorious MITI to its foreign counterparts), which manipulates business through its administrative guidance, seems to have a kind of corporate directorship over the whole Japanese economy. As the spokesman of big businesses, the Federation of Economic Organizations (Keidanren) represents about a thousand major companies and a hundred trade associations. Its president and committees have considerable infuence on government policy. The Japan Chamber of Commerce, representing medium-size and small businesses, also has some influence on the government. The Japanese Federation of Employers Association (Nikkeiren), with much the same membership as Keidanren, deals largely with labor-management relations in defense of the national economy. There are also organizations for smaller businesses (shopkeepers, farmers, fishermen, and so on) which ensure that the message of each particular group gets through.

Another administrative mechanism which is even more effective in supporting the functions of "Japan Incorporated" is the central government's system of transferring leading officials to high posts in the rural sector or to related private organizations. This custom in personnel administration is called *amakudari* (literally, "descending from heaven") and is similar to the practice in the Tokugawa period of appointing officials in Edo to posts in rural fiefs. Leading bureaucrats are usually graduates of the most prestigious universities, especially Tokyo University, who have qualified for their posts through the Higher Civil Servants Examinations. They are officials with a bright future and constitute a truly elite corps—apparently the cream of the Japanese educational system.

Shortly after their appointment, most of these young, promising elites are promoted to section chief. Only a few unfortunates are assigned simply to "chief" posts of subagencies or related branch offices. When some section chiefs are subsequently promoted to department managers, their remaining peers are shipped off to important posts in rural governments or subsidiary agencies, or even to private companies. The same action takes place when a limited number of department managers are promoted to bureau directors, and when one from among the bureau directors finally reaches the top bureaucratic post of vice minister. Through this series of eliminations, the vertical society maintains the necessary staff at various levels, with some elite officials disposed to rural posts at each step. The transfer of officials is partially the "right of the promoted"—to keep their rivals off the ladder—but more important, it is an unwritten rule of the vertical society that both winners and losers should not be made uncomfortable by having to be in the same office.

There is another form of *amakudari* which ties the bureaucrats even more closely to business. A bureaucrat who has looked after an industrial circle and therefore become familiar with it will be brought into a certain company after he has retired (or upon early retirement) as an adviser or counselor. This business strategy is designed mainly to utilize the former bureaucrat's connections with the ministry. In Japan, connections are the key to the social game. Through these transferred higher civil servants, who are scattered all over Japan as decision makers or wire pullers of a decision-making circle, the central government reinforces its links with the local governments and industries, smoothes administrative operations, and exercises vigilant watch over local activities, much as the Bakufu did in the Tokugawa era. The official connections netted by this system are largely responsible for the smooth working of "Japan Incorporated" and its fine synchronization of economic efforts. Even politicians of the ruling party sometimes take advantage of this nationwide system to collect electoral votes.

Subcontracting Systems

Still another social structure that makes "feudalistic capitalism" so vigorous is the pyramid-style subcontracting system. Most of the large Japanese firms operate in several locations, and they are eager to locate their head offices in Tokyo—near the headquarters of "Japan Incorporated," near the sources of capital and credit, and near the labor market of good, educated workers. A head office usually controls several plants, one or two laboratories, and a dozen sales offices, which are scattered throughout the country. Each local manufacturing plant usually hires a number of subcontractors in the area to produce the necessary components for assembling its final products. In addition, each subcontractor usually has several secondary subcontractors to carry out the production of semifinished parts. The secondary subcontractors, in turn, rely on small manufacturers to take on the preliminary stage of production. Sometimes even those tertiary subcontractors make use of outside hands, and the system goes down the line further. It is not unusual, at the bottom of the system, to find cottage industries and family enterprises that produce very small parts like pins, pegs, screws, and nuts, to be fitted into the products assembled at upper levels.

This system, which is not uncommon in Europe and America, contributes to a profitable business operation as defined by the difference between output and the cost of producing that output. But in Japan, there is greater emphasis on cost reduction and mutual dependence. The parent firm issues work orders to its child firm simply to get something done at lower cost; in turn, the child firm secures subcontracting work on a regular basis to get the job done. The survival of both parent and child are interlocked. In this system the cost of production decreases as the work flows downward, but the quality of products decreases as well. At the bottom of the pyramid it is extremely hard to expect production in quality as well as quantity. As a result, it is important for a parent company to install a safety valve for checking errors or substandard products. The safety valve could be materials supply, production know-how, or technical guidance on the job. The parent company willingly teaches its child firm the techniques needed to improve its limited capabilities. In addition, the higher-level subcontractors try to motivate people at the lower levels, particularly the top management of the lower subcontractors. At the higher levels success depends more than anything on the motivation of human minds, whereas at the lower levels timely cash payments are usually the best psychological incentive.

This hierarchical production system has given Japan a great competitive edge in coping with fluctuations in the economy and overcoming price wars. The large firms at the top usually get the lion's share of the profits, while the producers at the bottom receive a smaller share and are apt to go bankrupt in times of recession. But the parent company usually indicates its long-range production plan to the subcontractors and in recession caters to any crisis they may face. This is *giri* (socially interrelated duty). Thus the whole system of "feudalistic capitalism" is run by a large familylike group that makes the most of human labor.

In this chapter, I have stated briefly the historical and cultural distinctions of Japanese society. The following two chapters explore the characteristics of the people and the domestic institutions constituting that society.

2

THE "SELF"
OF THE JAPANESE

Japan has a fairly long north-south geographical extension, and is favored by four distinct seasons. It is natural that the people, after thousands of years as a homogeneous group blessed with the turn of the seasons, should develop a distinctive esthetic sense and a culture of sensitive emotions.

For the Japanese, the world was limited to their own islands. As a monolingual, racially homogeneous people, they cultivated their own social ideals of mutual duty and human feeling. The Japanese have traditionally depended upon each other a great deal. A reluctance to clearly assert oneself or to reject others arose naturally from the desire to maintain the cohesiveness of the isolated island society. An uneasiness when separated from the group also developed from this social ideal. The Japanese endeavored by mutual support to provide for what was lacking. In this system of mutual dependence, logic is reduced to a secondary principle, and efficiency often has to be sacrificed to the cause of agreement.

The Japanese have created a nonlogical social environment. "Nonlogical" is entirely different from "illogical." Nonlogical refers to a social approach based on the reality of human relationships rather than on abstract principles of human behavior.

Parliamentary democracy, jet airplanes, bullet trains, sky-high buildings, overseas tours—the Japanese today have all these sophisticated and efficient things, all the trappings of modern civilization. But this should not lead us to conclude that the Japanese people are completely modernized. The "self" of the Japanese is still tied to and nourished by the cultural traditions of the past. The jet airplanes, bullet trains, and sky-high buildings are only the physical additives of modern civilization; no chemical change seems to have taken place in the people themselves.

To understand the basic nature of the people, we should look more closely at the unique feature of the "self" that sustains Japanese society and see how it acts and reacts in response to the conditions of modern life. In Japanese society people must always select a persona appropriate to their role and perform in that persona on the social stage. They must hide beneath that mask. But a mask it remains. It is manipulated by the wearer, and the society functions as the aggregate of the masks. Let us see how a Japanese places himself into the mold or role prescribed by society.

Presentation of the Self

There are a great many ways of indicating the first-person singular ("I") in Japanese—from *watakushi* and *watashi* on to *atai, ore, boku, washi, temae, sessha, soregashi*, and including local variants such as *oidon* and pronounciation variants such as *wacchi*. The list seems to be endless. In English there is only "I," in French, "je," and in German, "Ich," in their various grammatical forms. Even the related languages of Chinese and Korean do not have as many expressions for the first-person singular. As far as I know, there is only one in Chinese and three in Korean. Compared with other countries, then, Japan has rich and varied modes for expressing the self.

This indicates the fine "distinctions of sentiment" that are often made in Japanese society, where the self takes on different forms by adapting to its environment. In other words, the word for the self is chosen with regard to a person's social role. When a samurai calls himself *sessha* (meaning "this clumsy one in humble modesty"), it is entirely appropriate; but if a merchant were to refer to himself by the same designation, it would seem extremely odd. Women do not refer to themselves as *ore* (an extremely masculine, relatively rough term for "I"), and children do not call themselves *washi* (a term used by old men). Again, these distinctions of sentiment are related to social position. A Japanese chooses the word for the self that best expresses his social status, preserves his place in society, and follows the hierarchical order of the social system.

The preservation of this delicate cultural expression is the manner in which the Japanese assign value to the self. Today the flood of modern civilization is bringing the doctrine of efficiency into Japan with great force. But even if the people's love of convenience leads them to devote their lives to the new ideal of efficiency, these intangible qualities of Japanese life are not likely to diminish.

Hanko Instead of Signature

It is said that the custom of using thumbprints to identify people derived from the blood compacts made by samurai warriors. The thumbprint further developed into the *hanko* (a stamp engraved with the Chinese characters for a person's name), which is used everywhere in Japan today. Even though Japan has entered the company of the advanced industrialized nations, there is no sign that the signature is taking the place of the *hanko*. A wave of internationalization has flooded into the lives of the Japanese people, but the custom of using the *hanko* shows no sign of diminishing. The stamp is placed on every important document in daily life, as the representation of the self.

The Japanese people are fond of symbols. The nation as a whole has the Emperor as its symbol, every company has its logo, and each family has a family crest that has been handed down from generation to generation. The symbol of the individual is the *hanko*. But in most cases, only the family name is engraved on the *hanko*. In other words, even though it represents the individual, it depicts him as a member of the family group. In addition, the family name on the *hanko* is always enclosed in a border, just as the self is enclosed within the social unit. In both these respects—the eternal relationship with the family and the enclosure of the individual within the family group—the *hanko* symbolizes the self of the Japanese.

In Europe and America, Southeast Asia, the Middle East and Africa, people always sign their names. So too, in trading companies like Mitsubishi and Mitsui, letters sent to other countries are signed. But all domestic correspondence and paperwork are stamped with the *hanko*. When employees of these companies were asked about this dual practice, they commented: "When we sign our name to something, sign our full name by our own hand, we feel as if the document is an individual responsibility and that we personally are offering the information. However, when we put our *hanko* on some papers that have been prepared by a typist, our own name is just a representation of the group, and using the *hanko* makes us feel more like it's a group project." This casual explanation is not far from the point.

In an ordinary Japanese household, the wife stamps the *hanko* of her husband on forms from the ward office or the tax bureau. She uses it even when she withdraws money from the bank. Since only the family name is inscribed on the *hanko*, it is very useful for all members of the household. In Western society, people use personal checks, which they validate with their signatures. Perhaps the popularity of the *hanko* is the reason personal signatures are not officially used in Japan. People do write personal checks, but they validate them with the *hanko*. The stamp is eminently useful in a group-oriented, cooperative society, and for that reason is unlikely to fall out of favor.

In a society where the group is the social core, consensus is extremely important. As an expression of consensus, a series of stamped *hanko*, all arranged in the proper hierarchical order, can be more effective than a series of signatures. The more *hanko* that appear on a document, the easier it is to process the document in a consensus-oriented society. Of course, the effort to collect as many *hanko* as possible leads to an extremely inefficient "administration by *hanko*." Although the system consolidates the strength of the group, it slows down decision making considerably. Furthermore, no single person feels special responsibility for the final action. Everyone tends to cooperate, but at the same time a person can shift responsibility to another's shoulders. Nevertheless, the *hanko* remains an integral part of the machinery of the government bureaucracy and of post offices, banks, real estate agencies—anywhere public business is carried on.

In the West, a stamp of a signature is sometimes used when the inefficiency of signing a large number of documents is too great. In this case, of course, there is no circle or border enclosing the signature. The stamp is simply a convenience, not an expression of the self. In the border enclosing the *hanko* is symbolized the special "closedness" of Japanese society and the way it encircles the individual. The Japanese live by depending upon each other in their closed system and have little desire to escape from this protective environment. This is why the lifetime employment system enjoys such great popularity in Japanese industry (see Chapter 4), and also why it is difficult for people to abandon the *hanko*.

Kao (Face)

It is well known that the Japanese word *kao* (face) refers not only to the physical features of the face but also to the totality of the individual. In fact, its use in the latter connotation is extremely common. The expression "He crushed my face" (*Kao-o tsu bushita*) means, of course, that someone has insulted my integrity; the expression "He flung mud in my face" (*Kao-ni doro-o nutta*) has the same meaning. My face is my "self"—my reputation, my integrity.

In like manner, the common expression "a broad face" (*Kao-ga hiroi*) refers, not to the width of the physical face, but to the fact that the person in question has a great many acquaintances. Here the self that moves through society, and more specifically the channel through which that self moves, is broad and expansive, coming into contact with many other people. Because this "broad face" has extensive contact with others, it can be employed to resolve social difficulties that may arise between conflicting parties, or may act as a go-between in various kinds of social negotiation. As a result of such activities, the "broad-faced" person possesses a certain social voice, and as he exercises that voice to resolve conflicts and difficulties, his social power increases. For this reason, the Japanese refer to someone who has a voice in society or in a group—someone who is counted upon to resolve conflicts and harmonize personal and social relationships—as *kao-yaku* (the face role). The person who plays the face role in a group takes responsibility for representing the wills of many people and communicating their wishes collectively to the larger society. Naturally, this person comes to possess what is known as a *kao-pasu* (face pass). His recognition, or face pass, sometimes becomes a free meal ticket for him. His recognizability can also be of benefit to others, who "borrow his face" (*kao-o kariru*). It's a simple fact that in Japan borrowing the face of another—that is, taking along some sort of reference from a person with a recognized face—is much more effective than attempting to identify yourself with a calling card or a driver's license when you wish to be introduced to someone you do not know.

The Japanese also say, "Don't make a big face" (*Ōkina kao-o suruna*). The person with a "big face" is pushy; he says what he wants without any regard for the etiquette of the group. Of course, this pushy attitude is expressed with the person's entire presence, not just the face. But the word "face" is used because the expressions and wishes, the overweening self-confidence and aggressiveness of such a person are immediately apparent in his face. The face is the external manifestation of the self to the world.

The expressions "I can see by your face" and "It shows in your face" tell us that the face does reveal the inner self. Abraham Lincoln is reported to have said, "After forty a man becomes responsible for his own face." Every passing day, the sufferings, the worries, the efforts, the joys, and the ambitions of each of us are engraved on our faces, creating the "face" that represents us to the world. It shows our character and our past. It is our living history, written in flesh. This is what Lincoln meant. Since the face is the living record of our growth and maturation, it is, for each and every one of us, the individual we are. The Japanese expression "He's got a good face" (*Ii kao-tsuki-o shiteru*) really means "He looks like an adult," or "He's masculine; he's tough." Those who excel in some art or those who have achieved a degree of recognition in professional sports have carefully cultivated this kind of "good face." The face is the self that people most seek to be proud of.

The Japanese also use the expressions "Won't you just show your face?" (*Kao-o misete kurenaika*) and "Could you lend me your face?" (*Kao-o kashite kurenaika*). These expressions mean simply "Won't you come?" and "Can you be there?" Again, such expressions refer to the person in his totality, but the word "face" is used to give a personal, emotional touch to the request. Japanese gangsters often use the expression "Give us your face!" (*Kao-o kase*), which is an order to come. The phrase has an extremely threatening effect because of the gut response that statements with the word "face" call up for the Japanese.

A few more examples: "It will involve my face" (*Kao-ni kakawaru*), meaning "It will damage my reputation"; "for the sake of my face" (*kao-ni menjite*), meaning "for my sake"; "to sell the face" (*kao-o uru*), meaning "to sell oneself"; and "an impressive line-up of faces" (*sōsōtaru kao bure*), meaning "an impressive gathering." These and many other expressions reveal that in everyday Japanese speech the word "face" is in some ways a substitute pronoun for the self. It represents the individual's honor, his social position, and his character. "Face" in the emotionally charged Japanese language contains the notion of self directed toward others.

Hara (Belly)

If *kao* (face) represents the outer aspect of the Japanese personality, *hara* (belly, or stomach) represents the inner self. This is not the physical stomach, as in the expressions "My stomach is empty" (*Hara ga suita*) and "beer belly" (*taiko hara*), but a conceptual "stomach," as in the expression "Let's spill our guts and talk" (*Hara o watte hanasō*). This means, "Let's present ourselves naked and talk, without hiding any of our thoughts or feelings from each other." The expression "He has stomach" (*Hara no aru otoko da*) implies that he has courage, that he's a person to be reckoned with. "My stomach is set" (*Hara wa kimatte iru*) expresses the subject's firm conviction about something, and conveys a picture of an immovable self. "My stomach is standing" (*Hara o tatete iru*) means that I am irritated, angry, or upset. In the classical Japanese essay "Tsurezure-gusa," by Yoshida Kenko, we find this passage: "If you don't speak your mind, your stomach will swell." Kenko is describing the anguish of keeping something inside and the consequences it can have for the inner self. When we express our anger, our face becomes contorted; but when we hold our anger in, our stomach becomes contorted, or "swollen." Of course, the physical stomach does not become swollen. It is the psychological or emotional self that suffers. Stomach refers to that self.

To have a "black stomach" means to be plotting something evil, to have a bad disposition, or to be in a perverse mood. When the Japanese say, "He's got a black stomach" (*Aitsu wa hara-ga kuroi*), they mean the person is crafty or is plotting treachery, and "stomach" refers to his inner intention.

The opposite expression is "His stomach is clean" (*Hara ga kirei*). This signifies that a person's nature is pure and noble, he is unable to perform a dishonorable or wicked act. It describes, of course, the self inside him. Therefore, "We can see through the stomach" (*Hara ga sukete mieru*) means "We can see through him"—we know what he's up to.

From the above we can conclude that "stomach" represents the interior self, with the strong implication that there is some part of that inner self that we wish to hide. For example, the expression "Can't you read my stomach?" (*Ore no hara ga yomenai noka*) implies that we want our partner to intuit our feelings, feelings we don't wish to express more directly. In this case, "stomach" refers to our intentions, and deep within these intentions lies the self that we do not wish to reveal.

From this concept of "stomach" developed *haragei* (the art of intuitive communication), a concept peculiar to Japan. The dictionary defines *haragei* as the expression that an actor puts into his performance—the psychological acting apart from the lines and gestures. These days, however, the term is used largely to describe the communications of politicians who, with dramatic gestures and vague catchwords, manage their political affairs. Among close associates in Japan, communication often takes place without complete verbalization. This is also known as communication by intuition, and it is an established mode of communication between husband and wife, daughter-in-law and mother-in-law, children and parents. This *haragei*—nonverbal, nongestural, intuitive communication—is the masterpiece of Japan's particularly emotional brand of human interaction.

Hara is the internal self, and for all purposes the real self. Further, this *hara*—the self that the person does not want to show to others—is his real intention *(honne)*, while his face *(kao)* is his public front *(tatemae)*. This double structure of the self— the face and the stomach, *kao* and *hara*—is treated in greater detail later in the chapter.

In summary, then: (1) In the emotional Japanese context, direct self-expression is frowned upon. In place of direct expression, various forms of indirect expression have evolved and are still employed. (2) *Kao* and *hara* are the most representative examples of these indirect forms of self-expression, and they refer to different aspects of the self—*kao* to the external, public self and *hara* to the internal, private intention.

Seppuku and Suicide

While we are on the subject of *hara*, it may be appropriate to discuss *seppuku* (literally, "cutting the belly"), popularly known as *harakiri* in the West. For this phenomenon, too, will help to reveal the nature of the self in Japan.

On the surface, *seppuku* would seem to be a self-destructive act, but that is not necessarily the case. Two kinds of *seppuku* must be distinguished. The first is *seppuku* as a punishment for a crime, and the second is the self-willed act. As a criminal sentence, *seppuku* has existed for hundreds of years as the ultimate punishment of the warrior class. The most famous case of this sort is of course the incident shaped into the Kabuki play *Chushingura,* written by Takeda Izumo (1691–1756), which tells the story of the revenge taken by 47 samurai.

In the shogun's castle at Edo, a *daimyō* named Asano Takuminokami wounded another lord named Kira Kozukeno- suke who had grossly insulted him. For this act Asano was sentenced to commit formal *seppuku.* As a result, all his subordi- nate samurai became unemployed. These 47 loyal *rōnin* (unem- ployed samurai), under the leadership of Oishi, made a plan to attack and kill Kira. The execution of the plan was not easy, since Kira was very much on his guard. But at last, early one snowy morning, Oishi and his followers stormed Kira's house in Edo and killed him. The shogun, Tsuneyoshi, sentenced the loyal 47 *rōnin* to the honorable suicide that he thought would meet both the requirements of public law and the real wishes of the *rōnin*—who must surely desire, having achieved their aim, to join their avenged lord in the next world. So Oishi and his men committed *seppuku*.

There can be nothing as barbaric as a punishment which forces a person to take his own life, and this is what *seppuku* is: the worst possible punishment for a crime. It is much more brutal and inhuman than the electric chair, the firing squad, or the gallows. For the hardy samurai class, however, it was not inappropriate. The Meiji Restoration abolished the samurai class and, accordingly, *seppuku* as a punishment for crime disappeared as well.

For the interest of readers, let me briefly describe the way *seppuku* is done. According to tradition, when a man performs *seppuku*, he has to be careful not to insert more than three-tenths of the blade into his stomach; otherwise, it would injure the bowels and cause him unbearable pain. The *seppuku* performer begins by putting a *sampō* (a wooden tray) under his hips so that he will fall frontward rather than die in an ignominious posture. The *sampō* has a stand on which a sword blade wrapped with white cloth or paper is set. The performer holds the blade by the wrapped portion, sets it to the left side of his stomach, and exhales. On inhaling, he inserts the blade (it goes in much easier than when he is exhaling) and then pulls it to the right side at a stroke.

The inserting and cutting described above do not lead to immediate death. So to die easily, the performer sets the blade against his carotid artery with his right hand and presses it down with his left hand to cut the artery. (He doesn't have to do this when a man whose role is called *kaishaku*—a second—is present. The second cuts off the head of the *seppuku* performer after he has cut his stomach himself.)

The other kind of *seppuku* is the self-willed act of annihilation, the destruction of the self without a formal sentence. But I would like to interpret this kind of *seppuku* as an attempt at self-assertion, an effort to liberate the self in glory when all other alternatives are blocked. When a person chooses *seppuku* as the only solution to an unsolvable dilemma, the decision derives not from self-denial but from a glorious self-affirmation. It is an attempt to express the glorious end of the self in the most unfavorable or disgraceful circumstances.

Let me give an example. The suicide of novelist Yukio Mishima, once a Nobel prize nominee, shocked the world. Mishima had formed his own militaristic group, *Tate-no-kai,* and was spreading rightist ideology. On November 25, 1970, taking the Director General of the Eastern Sector of the Self-Defense Forces as his hostage, he stepped out onto the balcony of the building and hailed the soldiers below to throw their lot in with him. When this failed, he decided to commit *seppuku* as a last resort. In order to demonstrate the strength of his determination, and to persuade the members of the Self-Defense Forces to follow him, he chose a glorious death by *seppuku*.

In the act of *seppuku* is revealed the unbending will of the self, a firm determination to face down the impasse that confronts it, and an almost arrogant will to triumph over it. *Seppuku* is the ultimate self-justification. Mishima's *seppuku* was just that, as is the *seppuku* of the soldier in the battlefield who refuses to surrender or be taken prisoner.

I was an officer in the Japanese Imperial Navy at the close of World War II. When the message of the Japanese surrender came through, one of our admirals gathered all the young officers and cadets in the lecture hall and instructed them earnestly about Japan's recovery. The next morning, news of the admiral's death by *seppuku* reached us. On the surface, this was merely a self-destructive act on the part of the admiral; but it was also a message of encouragement to us (at least every one of us felt so at the time). The message of the admiral's death was this: "As long as possible, I will preserve my integrity. Therefore I will die holding it." Again, this form of *seppuku* is a glorious means of self-expression. Unlike the form of *seppuku* used as a punishment for the samurai class, it is a matter not of self-denial but of self-affirmation.

Many foreigners have difficulty understanding this concept because they confuse *seppuku* with simple suicide. And they seem to think that whenever the Japanese commit suicide, they do it by *seppuku (harakiri)*. In fact, the Japanese usually commit suicide by taking pills or hanging themselves (private ownership of guns is prohibited). Nowadays, very few people have the determination to die by *seppuku*. When faced with impossible difficulties, only those with great strength of mind choose to die without surrendering to their opponent, or make no attempt to escape but rather affirm the self and the will in a grand manner to the end by choosing *seppuku*. In contrast, simple suicide is only a means of escaping an impasse, of avoiding the immediate suffering at hand. The mind of the person who attempts *seppuku* is quite different. In the act of slashing the belly is symbolized the righteousness of the self.

Japan is known worldwide for its large number of suicides, but Sweden has an even greater number. When we compare the victims of suicides in these two countries, we find that the elderly make up the large majority of suicides in Sweden, whereas in Japan suicide is most frequent among the middle-aged. Lately in Japan suicides among people in their thirties and forties have increased. How can we explain these two phenomena?

As everyone knows, Sweden has one of the most complete social welfare systems in the world. The elderly are well provided for and suffer no lack of life's essentials. Their nursing homes are surrounded by greenery and seem like palaces to the Japanese experts who tour these facilities. The Japanese visitors are always greatly impressed with the luxury of the equipment and the setting, but it is reported that in those same luxurious facilities suicides are an all too frequent occurrence. Apparently, when people are placed in such surroundings, with a complete support system that frees them from any need or want, they lose their desire to live. Without any work to devote themselves to, without emotional contact with family and friends, they become increasingly alienated from and uninterested in this world. This is especially true for the elderly, who know what end faces them all too soon. There is no value in living if you are totally alone and isolated. As a result, many decide to hurry their death with their own hands.

These are people who have lived within the tradition of Western individualism. Individualists can survive only as long as they have a personal goal to challenge them, and an opponent to compete with. Without a goal that defines the self, without other people to offer a challenge, individualists don't feel "alive" even though they may be physically existing. Thus despite their independence, individualists cannot survive in isolation.

In contrast, suicide among the middle-aged in Japan seems to occur when, frustrated on all sides, the victim cannot find anyone who understands him well. The group-oriented Japanese tend to head in the direction of suicide when they lose a relationship with colleagues or a family member who will comfort them in their weakness and provide psychological support. A part of the self gives way when this support is withdrawn or denied, and suicide often follows.

Young people sometimes commit suicide because they have failed their entrance examinations. Others commit suicide because of disappointment in love. The Japanese thrive on mutual dependence. Anyone loses self-reliance in direct proportion to his degree of dependence on a group. The greater the degree of dependence encouraged by the group, the weaker a person's own desire for self-affirmation becomes, and the easier it is for him to feel hopelessly frustrated when he is excluded from the group. This form of social ostracism is known as *mura-hachibu*.

In conclusion, the high incidence of suicide among the elderly in Sweden is the bitter fruit of the individualist doctrine, the unfortunate result of losing a sense of self when one is isolated from the goals and challenges of life. In contrast, suicide among the middle-aged in Japan is the tragic result of a self that has been spoiled by excessive dependence on the group or on support from the family.

Mieppari (Self-Display)

It was a windy day in Yokohama. As a friend and I were walking down the street, we came across a fellow on a scaffold painting a signboard. The scaffold was swaying in the wind and the painter was hanging on with all his might. Out of concern, my friend walked under the signboard. He was surprised to discover that he knew the acrobatic painter. "Hey! Don't you think you'd better leave that work to someone a little younger? It's dangerous. Why don't you come on down?" The old man shouted back: "Even in a city as large as Yokohama, I'm the only one who could paint a signboard in a wind like this!"

If it were merely pride of workmanship that motivated this painter, he would not have had to expose himself to such danger. No. This was a fierce *mieppari* (act of self-display). According to the dictionary, the first half of the word, *mie*, means "the act of being conscious of another person and trying to show oneself off to best advantage before him." This is not necessarily a bad thing. "I am the only one capable of doing this, no other painter would dare it, I am a superior painter"—such was the message the old man was eager to convey. This is *mieppari*, or "display of the self."

The wife of a certain family goes shopping. She checks her daily spending account and decides that the only dish the family can afford that day is mackerel (a relatively inexpensive fish) and that mackerel will have to do. But on the way to the market she meets another woman from the same company housing quarters, and by the time she gets to the store the mackerel she had intended to buy has become tuna (a much more expensive purchase). She found it impossible to buy mackerel in front of another woman of the same social rank. Her "honor as a woman" was at stake. "Honor" is an inner dictum, an internal standard of conduct. When it was manifested externally in this case, it became display. In Japan, honor and pride are intimately connected with the place one occupies in the social hierarchy. To avoid sacrificing her honor, the housewife bought the tuna, though not without a sigh and an ironic smile to herself. Maybe she will be able to balance the books next time.

Display of this sort in Japan is a response to the rigid social hierarchy. It is, in a way, an act of resistance, or at least of battling to assert one's true place in that order. If the woman who wanted to buy mackerel had been a department head's wife and the woman she met on the way had been of lower rank, she would have been even less likely to buy the mackerel. For the honor of "Mrs. Department Head" it would have been necessary to buy not just tuna but prime fillet of tuna. The housewife is under this stricture whether or not she is shopping with someone else. As long as she thinks, "Someone might see me, and anyway that fishmonger is liable to talk," she would not consider touching the mackerel. The reason that mackerel and another inexpensive fish, the sardine, sell poorly in Japan is because they don't contribute to this fierce contest to display status.

Japan is a rank-conscious society, and each person lives under the careful scrutiny of every other member. No one wants to be bested. If one family puts up a pole with carp-shaped banners (done in Japan for the sons of the family on the Boys'

Festival, May 5), you can be sure the next-door neighbors will raise a banner too, no matter what the expense would do to the family budget. "We can't be outdone" is the logic behind this eternal struggle for self-display.

In the 1960s, the three "magic appliances"—the electric refrigerator, the electric washer, and the television set—spread through the country like wildfire. This had nothing to do with any special efforts by appliance salesmen. All they had to do was say, "The people next door bought one," and the deal was closed. When one or two women are seen carrying a handbag made by some prestigious European firm, it's only a matter of months before hundreds of travelers bring back the same thing from their next trip to Europe. In no time at all the streets are full of women wearing "charmink" coats and parading the same hand-bag on their arm. This is called a woman's "miep-Paris." On a larger scale, it is an example of the problems posed by living in a hierarchical society where appearance is the standard by which one's place in the hierarchy is judged.

Self-display in Western society is a bit different. In the West, self-display is on a scale grander than mackerel and tuna, hand-bags and coats, or risking one's life in a violent wind to show how good one is at one's work. In the West, self-display often takes the form of "the bigger, the better." People build large swimming pools or purchase private aircraft or gorgeous yachts. It was a strong desire for self-display that motivated a certain billionaire to make a famous opera singer his wife, then leave her for the widow of an American President. He was, in effect, announcing to the world, "I can do anything!" His display was an attempt to assuage the wound of being excluded from the cream of society in spite of his great wealth. In short, display in the West is often used for struggle against the class system, while in Japan it is used for asserting one's place within the order of the hierarchy.

In earlier centuries, when Japan indeed had social classes, display served the purpose of class conflict there as well. In the

Tokugawa period, as stated before, all Japanese were divided into four classes: samurai, peasants, craftsmen, and merchants. The merchants, lowest on the scale, battled against the class system by many kinds of display. They lent large sums of money to the samurai and, if no repayment was made, received permission to carry small swords in return. They ransomed geisha—usually geisha who had fallen in love with some samurai—and, in general, lived a life of luxury.

Today the efforts of parents to get their sons into a first-rate university at whatever cost and the bright kimono that young women wear as the "unnecessary necessity" at their graduation ceremony or on Adults' Day are both manifestations of the struggle with the hierarchy. Of course, I am not saying that display is utterly without value. In fact, display is the moving force behind much of Japan's cultural and economic development.

The Blend Society

From the *han* (clans) of samurai, *za* (guilds) of merchants, and *kumi* (groups) of firefighters during the feudal period, to the modern "National Railway Family," the "home company" organization, and the various ministries of the government, there have been many sorts of organizations in Japan. The important point is that they are all social groups as well as bureaucratic or industrial organizations, and they have always displayed three traits.

These are (1) a *hierarchy* that forces the individual to define his own limits by his position in the order; (2) an *exclusivity* that prevents members of one group from identifying with members of another group; and (3) a *cohesiveness* that blends the members of each group into a uniform entity. These traits are aptly manifested in the modern industrial or bureaucratic organization in the form of the seniority system, the in-company union, and lifetime employment. Every "self" in Japan lives by, and is in fact created by, responding to these three traits, as illustrated in part in Chapter 1.

The most important feature of the self in Japan is its dissolution into the group, as many scholars from various disciplines have pointed out. We are clearly reminded here of the ancient Buddhist and Confucian concepts of losing one's identity by merging with the larger entity through enlightenment. But the most significant point is that dissolution of the self is essentially an act of will—of self-control and self-discipline—that is, the quality control of individual emotions.

Japan is a "blend" society. Just as barley loses its original nature when each grain is blended to make whiskey, so the blending and dissolution of each individual in Japanese society produces a new social energy and activity. The Japanese are perhaps the most successful people in the world when it comes to working in groups. This remarkable cohesion accounts for Japan's ability to reach a high level of industrialization in such a short time and, more recently, to survive the oil crisis. The reverse side of the coin—the price of strong cohesion—is of course the weakness of individual development that is often cited by foreign observers.

In contrast, in the West the self endeavors to survive on its own, even though it participates in the larger group. Here the self is like a single tile in a mosaic. In a mosaic composition, various shades of blue tiles are grouped together to create the sky; many different shades of red tiles are arranged to depict a red robe. Each tile retains its unique shape and color while forming part of the whole. So it is in the West. Each individual lives by emphasizing and expressing his uniqueness within the social order. The self is not lost. This is what I call the "mosaic" society.

Of course, there are good and bad mosaics, and there are

social groups that function well and those that function poorly. The same can be said for blends of whiskey and people. Daniel Bell and Ezra F. Vogel, in their article "The Possibility of Japan" (published in the *Asahi Evening News*), coined the terms "sand society" and "clay society." The former refers to Western societies that have little coherence and that place strong emphasis on individualism. The latter refers to Japan's extremely cohesive social composition. This interesting distinction resembles the division into "mosaic" and "blend" societies I have described above.

Many foreigners complain that no matter how long they live in Japan they are never really accepted by the Japanese and never admitted into the society. This may be partly due to the insularity of the Japanese, who have lived as a homogeneous island nation for centuries. But it is not simply a matter of exclusivity or xenophobia. Rather, especially from the viewpoint of the Japanese, it is a problem of blending. The assumption that foreigners can never truly blend in may derive from the fact that in a group of black-haired people, someone with brown hair simply does not fit in.

On a more meaningful level, someone who has a firm notion of self, with all the logical implications that such a notion entails, cannot be expected to lose that self and enter into the group-oriented Japanese society, which is governed not by logic but by the social principles of *giri* (mutual duty) and *ninjō* (human feeling). If that alien element were to take root in Japanese society, its cohesion could only suffer. Another factor may be the sympathy of the Japanese for a foreigner, their reluctance to force the outsider to give up his individual identity in order to blend into Japanese society. Thus the foreigner is forever treated as a guest, with all the etiquette that is demanded when greeting and entertaining a visitor from afar.

Very few Japanese believe that foreigners should be absorbed into Japanese society, at the cost of their individualism.

Again, this is not due to an ill-natured xenophobia. Here, by the way, let me add a note about the term *gaijin* (outsider, foreigner), an abbreviation for the longer *gaikokujin* (person from another country). Unlike the English term "Jap," *gaijin* is definitely not a term of insult. The English "Jap" can be traced back to the wartime animosity between the two countries and is perhaps equivalent to the Japanese *ketō* (literally, "hairy Chinese"—a disparaging term applied to the Chinese and later to all foreigners).

The ancient name for Japan is Yamato, meaning "Great Harmony," and as already stated the highest social ideal of the Japanese people is *wa* (harmonious concord). The following is an example of how the principle of harmony governs a modern samurai's behavior. It is a testimony by a member of one of the top-level companies in Japan:

"During inventory there was a great deal of work to be done, and I worked overtime for several days, even on the weekends. After it eased off a bit, I decided to take a day off that was owed me. But while at home, I felt very uneasy because I was away from the company. Still, it would have looked silly for me to show up when I had taken the day off. I invented some lame excuse and made a telephone call to the company, but there didn't seem to be anything special requiring my attention. That evening, I went to the station to buy the evening paper, and I bumped right into a horde of office workers coming out of the ticket gate on their way home from work. When I saw them, I suddenly felt as if I had done something wrong that day, and I couldn't get away from the guilty feeling all night."

This is the conscience of the well-blended individual, of the self that has been harmonized into Japanese society. I call such a diligent worker a "modern samurai" because he devotes himself wholeheartedly to his employer and always puts his official duty first—much as the samurai devoted themselves to their lord in the Tokugawa period. What this story reveals is not exactly the "shame" that Ruth Benedict discusses in her book *The Chrysan-themum and the Sword,* but rather a sense of guilt. In any case, in Japan both shame and guilt are derived from the same root—heteronomy, or lack of personal freedom.

"Not for Myself"

There are scandals in Japan as in any human society, and those involving corrupt relations between the public and private sectors are particularly reprehensible. But one thing is different in Japan. In every case, those implicated in the scandals feel compelled to profess their selfless motives. After they have testified before the committee, or finished an investigative session with the authorities, and face questions at the inevitable press interview, they all pull themselves up proudly and deliver the same line: "Nothing I did was for personal gain. It was not for myself."

The Japanese claim they did what they had to do for the sake of the company or the party. They say that they had no choice but to act as they did—it was a matter of survival. The executive director of one trading company, who was implicated in an aircraft scandal, committed suicide and left a note which read, in part, "It wasn't me." If it wasn't him, we may ask, why did he find it necessary to take his own life? The indirect answer is to be found in another part of that note: "The company is eternal." It is almost as if loyalty to the company made any consideration of personal blame irrelevant, even inconceivable. The director's "self" was dissolved into the eternal company.

The other day, a letter entitled "An Upsetting Interview" appeared in a local newspaper. In it, a college student described what happened to a friend of his who had taken the entrance test for employment at a bank in his hometown. The bank interviewer was openly rude to the applicant: "Well, you were certainly lucky to get into college for someone who graduated from X high school. Hmmm. It looks like all your school courses are in law and government. Certainly nothing here is related to banking." The student was indignant at the way his friend was treated. But what interested me most was the following remark: "My friend was very angry at being treated in this way, and was about to reply in the same tone, but checked himself. He thought of all the future graduates of his high school who might someday want to apply for a job at this bank, and decided not to answer back but instead to put up with the treatment he was receiving." This concern for "the future graduates" transcended momentary personal considerations.

It is quite common in Japan for people to control their own behavior after considering its possible effect on their peers, or their juniors. If the student applying for employment at the bank had not controlled himself, the interviewer would no doubt have come to the conclusion that all the graduates of X high school were as inferior as he suspected. In Japan the members of a group are strung together like the beads of a rosary, and in most cases individual responsibility becomes collective responsibility. This collective self, made up of a string of individuals, and the collective responsibility they share, is a major feature of civilian society in Japan.

The first group that a child becomes a member of is the *ie* (family, house). From the earliest moment of awareness, the child is taught to behave in a way that will not injure the family's reputation: "You'll be laughed at if you do that." "We want you to study hard and be the best—do you understand?" These are just two examples of the admonitions that soon become familiar to the child. For the sake of the family's reputation, all sorts of expectations and pressures are heaped on this small "self."

In Japan it is not unusual for collective responsibility to continue long after the child has become an adult. If, for example, the son of a certain family were to rob a bank, all the members of his family would be held responsible by the society for the son's violation of its rules. This is not, of course, a legal responsibility; rather, it is a social responsibility that falls on all members of the *ie*. In the West, provided that his family were not accomplices, the bank robber and the bank robber alone would be ostracized by society and punished by law.

The "rosary" of collective responsibility sometimes extends beyond the family chain. For example, district and municipal police chiefs often resign from their posts when one of their underlings commits a crime, even if it is strictly of an individual nature. The executive director mentioned previously, while saying "It wasn't me," committed suicide because he was so entangled in the web of collective responsibility of his company. The proud, almost self-righteous "Nothing I did was for personal gain" before the committee and the self-effacing "I thought of all the future graduates" at the job interview may have different results, but they derive fundamentally from the same impulse. They are the cries of an individual straining under the burden of collective responsibility, a burden which is often too heavy for the individual to bear.

Osusowake (Sharing)

In Japan a person who monopolizes his crops in a group is the object of intense criticism, just as a person who monopolizes a public gain receives his share of angry stares and cold looks. Even someone who attempts to monopolize a private achievement within a group receives this treatment. In Japanese society the credit for private ownership of anything of value usually belongs to the group.

If, for example, a student attempts to take personal credit for words of praise from his teacher or refuses to share the glory of some academic achievement, he will almost certainly be treated coldly by his fellow students. In a Japanese business company, there is no star. Companies don't make stars. The semiannual company bonus is, in principle, evenly distributed among all employees in proportion to their rank in the hierarchy. Employees are not considered members of a baseball team, where some might be stars and others "utility players." Rather, they are members of a tug-of-war—each has an equal weight to pull.

A better example: A company worker in Nagano prefecture drew the winning ticket in a lottery totaling ¥10,000,000 (about $43,500). He was so excited over his good fortune that he talked about it to his fellow workers. That was his undoing. From then on his relationship with his co-workers deteriorated, and an underlying current of hostility made it very difficult for him to work with them as he had before. What did he do? He stood up in front of the entire office staff, raised the ticket above his head, and waved it in the air so that all eyes were glued to the winning stub. Then he set it on fire with his cigarette lighter and reduced it to ashes, totally ignoring his fellow workers who cried out, "Hey, wait! Stop that! Don't be a fool!" He sacrificed the prize in a grand appeal to win back the favor of his cold-hearted co-workers and reestablish his original relationship with the group.

If, when he announced his luck to his fellows, he had offered to treat them all to an appropriately splendid meal, or even announced his decision to buy uniforms or some equipment for the company baseball team, perhaps there would have been no need for this drastic measure. But he did not know that he was not permitted to monopolize any fortune that came his way unexpectedly. The custom of *osusowake* (sharing; literally, "giving away the hem") is deeply ingrained in the group-oriented Japanese society. In this society the self is not recognized by the group at all unless it is totally dissolved into that group. And if the self is not recognized by the group, it has no value. This is the main reason that the Western notion of self has great difficulty gaining a foothold in Japan.

Let me give one more example of an individual "monopolizing" something from the Japanese point of view. Years ago, the wife of an American officer stationed at one of the bases of the occupation force won a ¥180,000 grand prize in the Officers' Club bingo game. At that time, ¥180,000 was equivalent to $500, a respectable sum even for an American. The family maid, who was Japanese, heard of this and was eagerly expecting some sort of *osusowake*. One day, two days, and finally a week passed with no hint of a gift forthcoming. The officer's wife was happy to receive this windfall and went about the house in a very cheerful mood, but the maid didn't receive so much as a new blouse as her share of the prize. This bothered her immensely, and she complained to the other maids in the neighborhood: "The woman I work for is a real skinflint. She won that grand prize, but she hasn't bought me a single thing!" The maid was merely venting the frustration of her disappointed expectation, but as a matter of course her complaint traveled round and round and found its way back to her employers. She was dismissed summarily and found herself out on the doorstep with her bags in hand.

From the maid's point of view, as a member of the household she was entitled to her share of all the good fortune and happiness that came to the family. Of course, this was simply a sort of *amae* (dependence) on her part, owing to the traditional Japanese family system. However, the wife thought only that it was money she herself had won, and that was that. Justifying her firing of the maid, she said, "Whether it's a windfall or not, there's no reason to spend it unless we have to." In a different culture, *osusowake* is simply not a legitimate reason for spending money.

There may be some differences here in how Americans and Japanese view money, but basically what is operating is the difference between the Japanese and the American view of privacy. The vast majority of people in Japan think of privacy as not entering another's room uninvited, or not prying into the secrets of another. The broader meaning of privacy—as "a private sphere separated from the group" with regard to time, space, thought, belief, and fortune or misfortune—is alien to the Japanese. The people have always lacked any concept of privacy as something that attaches value to the individual identity. The reason, once again, is that at the bottom of their hearts the Japanese believe the self is made whole by being dissolved into the group.

Medetai (Felicitations) and Omedetai (Naivete)

Everyone knows how much the Japanese enjoy festivals. The festivals were originally based on religious celebrations, but today people look for any excuse they can for fun and joviality. Weddings have been becoming more and more luxurious, and commemorative celebrations on the sixtieth birthday of distinguished Japanese personalities are also extremely popular. The things which are celebrated, then, are not limited to the gods or to heroes of ancient times. Anything will do. Anything is enough to set the Japanese off shouting, "*Medetai, Medetai!*" ("Felicitations!")

The word *medetai* originally applied to an event or an object that was worthy of devotion or adoration, and was uttered to express respect and praise for that event or object. Today it is used only to describe the happy, joyous feeling of the festival affairs.

In Japan, the most *medetai* time of all is the New Year. For the first three days of the New Year, the special New Year's *sake* (rice wine) flows abundantly, and everyone is bright and cheerful. "Sun becomes a god when it rises on the first day," goes the *senryu* (epigrammatic poem of 17 syllables). It is a fact of nature that the sun rises day after day in the eastern sky, but the Japanese consider that first sunrise of the year especially felicitous. On New Year's Day, people who normally never give a moment's thought to the gods are seen wearing their brightest kimono and flocking to the shrines in hordes. They offer their personal wishes for the coming year to the gods, snatch *omikuji* (sacred oracles) from a little wooden box, and scramble over one another to buy lucky "demon-banishing arrows." The whole scene illustrates the Japanese propensity to move around in crowds. They seem hardly able to find happiness outside a crowd.

In the olden days, people purified themselves on the first day of the New Year and dedicated the day to their determination to make a fresh start. In the expression "sunrise on the first day," their dreams and hopes for the year ahead were carried up into the sky. When people wished the gods to answer their prayers, they would do penance by walking back and forth before the shrine a hundred times with an offering of prayers, then purify themselves by repeated ablutions, offering their spirits to the gods. Nowadays they just follow a crowd and visit a shrine on New Year's Day, clapping their hands once or twice and giving the bell rope a yank while they toss in a ¥100 coin in the hope that their prayers will be answered by the gods.

The Japanese celebrate the first day of the year as before, but nowadays it is less a religious celebration than a time when their simple-heartedness brims to overflowing. Whatever they choose to do, or wherever they choose to go, they choose together and do together. They go through the New Year's ritual as if it were just another seasonal fashion. Perhaps the progress of civilization and science has blunted the hearts of the Japanese a bit. For whatever reason, few people today wholeheartedly celebrate the New Year in the true meaning of *medetai*.

Another *medetai* time for the Japanese people is the cherry-blossom season. In early spring the people traditionally hold a *sake* party under the fully bloomed cherry trees. They drink, sing, dance, and have a good time. The tradition dates back to the Tokugawa period, when a certain Kuma-san (Mr. Bear) and Hachi-san (Mr. Eight) got the idea of making money in this jovial setting by selling *sake*. They brought a *sake* barrel into the fields where the people were having a party in celebration of the blossoms. While waiting for a customer to come and buy *sake*, Kuma-san got thirsty and told his partner, "I want a cup of *sake*.

Here, I'll pay you five *mon* for the cup." (The denominations then were *mon* and *ryō* instead of sen and yen.) Hachi-san pocketed the money, but soon after that he also wanted a drink. "Now let me have some *sake*," he said. "Here is the money for the cup." He returned the five *mon* he had just received from Kuma-san. In due course, Kuma-san got thirsty again and paid back the five *mon* for a cup of *sake*. Thus the exchange of the same money went on and on and the sale of *sake* continued. When these two *omedetai* (naive) chaps closed down for the day, only five *mon* and the empty *sake* barrel were left.

This anecdote is known as "Economy of *Sake* over the Cherry-Blossom Party" in Japan. Here we might think of the world economy emptying the oil barrel or depleting the mountains of natural resources. Is that, too, not *omedetai*?

The dictionary defines *omedetai* as the quality of a person "who is credulous to the point of being simple; easily fooled by others." The naivete of the Japanese derives in part from their insularity—from the fact that they have lived for centuries in a self-enclosed circle of dependence.

Whether Pearl Harbor was a surprise attack or a cleverly laid trap for the Japanese is still much debated, though almost 40 years have passed since the end of the war. In this regard, Shinoda Yujiro, professor at Sophia University, has stated, "Japan was drawn into a trap. . . . Roosevelt forced the Japanese to make the first strike in order to smash all opposition in Congress and from the American people. To this end, Japan served his purposes well" (*Shimaguni to Nipponjin: The Japanese and Their Island Country*). If Professor Shinoda's conclusion is justified, the Japanese truly were, in this case, tragically naive and foolish.

Wabi and Sabi

Wabi and *sabi* are two widely known emotional values in Japanese culture. They lie in exactly the opposite spiritual direction from *medetai* and *omedetai*. They describe the states of mind of a person who seeks to retire from society, who values solitude and loves quietness. His back firmly turned away from the expression of joyful communal feeling, the seeker of *wabi* and *sabi* pursues a transcendental life. It is said that neither word has a proper equivalent in any foreign language. To explain *wabi* and *sabi* as states of loneliness is erroneous. Their adjectival forms, *wabishii* and *sabishii*, which represent the road that leads to *wabi* and *sabi*, suggest a sort of "lonely sadness" and "isolated sadness," but those who have traveled that road and reached true *wabi* and *sabi* are not afflicted by loneliness. Rather, they experience a oneness with all that surrounds them.

The reader may be familiar with this feeling, but I would like to give a few examples. Here are two famous *haiku* (17-syllable poems with an element suggesting a season) by Issa (1763–1827) of the Tokugawa period:

> Don't give up, little frog; Issa is here with you.
> Come and play with me, orphan sparrow!

Both of these *haiku* describe a solitary state of mind, but there is no element of loneliness in them. The transcendent figure of Issa, blended in with his surroundings, is magnificently alive in these poems. This is *wabi* and *sabi*, states of mind in which a solitary person preserves his identity and reveals it.

In February of 1979, ten previously missing poems by Issa were found in Nagano prefecture. Let me quote a few:

> In this field of graves, a cockscomb blooms alone.

The cockscomb represents Issa, of course. The cockscomb blooming in its fierce individuality may seem lonely, but it has transcended its lonely environment (the graveyard) and while dissolving into its surroundings manages to exhibit its own identity.

> If the *ominaeshi* flowers happen to hate me,
> I will make the moon my friend.

The *ominaeshi* represents the female form (there is a visual suggestion of this in the Chinese characters used to write the flower's name). This *haiku* describes the state of mind of a transcendental man who has left the love of women behind him. Here is another:

> This stone Jizo in the weeds
> Receives the blessings—these blooming grasses.

Wabi and *sabi* are not the dried-up states of a solitary hermit. There remains a sympathetic spirit that respects the abandoned statue of Jizo (a Buddhist saint) and assigns it offerings as well. Issa is actually enjoying his transcendent state of singleness and isolation, because he identifies with the universe around him. Here the self is not "sad" at all, but is rejoicing in its surroundings.

Does a businessman who is slaving away day after day have time to experience this kind of transendent state and identification with the universe? Or is his self lost, wandering aimlessly with no certain path? Of course, in the midst of modern society, it is extremely difficult to preserve a sense of solitude and to experience the states of *wabi* and *sabi*. Yet it is not impossible. *Wabi* and *sabi* are not the exclusive possessions of the poets. These states of being are available to all of us, as the next anecdote demonstrates.

"After I became president of the company, my personality changed completely. Everything—the trust and confidence of the business world in our company, the enthusiasm and reliability of the workers—rested with me. For this reason, I was forever busy with this and that, and there was no room for error on my part. I had to plunge right into all sorts of difficult personnel decisions and other kinds of extremely complex business, with no one to cover for me or to take the blame if I botched things up. After spending days considering some particularly difficult problem and finally arriving at a decision, I would be overcome by a great loneliness and depression. There seemed to be no way to escape it, no way out. To repair my frayed nerves and release some of the stress that had built up inside me, I changed my lifestyle completely.

"I opted for the simple life. I tried to find joy and pleasure in the daily chores of living. Though I used to enjoy drinking and going to parties with hostesses at a club, I gave up night life entirely. It took a long time for me to find any pleasure in my new lifestyle.

"In our inexpensive house in the suburbs, there is a little four-and-one-half mat room [approximately eight square meters]. I can take whatever is bothering me—my worries or my depression—with me into that room and close the door behind me. There I can read a book if I like, I can write, I can watch television, or just give myself up to the wanderings of my imagination. I can take a nap, or serve myself some tea. Since I don't allow anyone else into this room, my little four-and-one-half mat space is my castle, my favorite place in the world.

"I am very glad to have a place like this. Fortunately, there are lots of trees on the property. It's quiet. When the weather is nice I sit on the veranda and enjoy passing my time just watching the little garden. These may seem like the pleasures of an old man, but this quiet time of my own makes me more effective in fighting the battles I must fight at work, and in leading my 'troops' energetically."

In spite of his busy and demanding public life, this remarkable businessman has managed to achieve inner peace and harmony. In Japan, a heroic person has mastery over the affairs of this world and also displays a sensual "self" that dazzles those around him. Those who aim at *wabi* and *sabi* refine themselves to the highest degree by retreating to a quiet environment and allowing their "self" to merge with their surroundings. Though submerged, the essential individuality of the self gallops free. It is this state that has attracted so many Westerners to Zen.

The Defeat of Vending Machines

The story is an old one. When a major supermarket chain opened the first fully mechanized supermarket in Japan, it placed 67 vending machines in an area of 800 square meters. The machines offered the customer over 250 different products, mostly foodstuffs. All the customer had to do was press a button, and his purchase would drop down into his hands. The company had recently streamlined its distribution system and prided itself on being in the forefront of commercial development. However, customers absolutely refused to patronize the store. The closing of this supermarket almost immediately after it opened attracted nationwide attention and forced the company to reconsider the direction in which it was heading.

In a survey carried out by the chain, customers were asked why they refused to patronize the store. They replied that there was no one to talk to, and that the whole shopping experience "lacked a feeling of personal relationships." Even though the automated supermarket was an efficient labor-saving device, it was extremely inefficient when it came to satisfying customers. The Japanese people need emotional ties with others; they need to be part of a group.

These days mechanization seems to extend to every aspect of society, to people as well as things. Even schoolteachers have become like vending machines. They dispense mechanical lectures after their salary is "inserted" into the machine. But people, especially young people, cannot live in an emotional vacuum. Even if they have shelter and clothing and vending machines to supply all their food and drink—even their entertainment and education—with everything clunking out at the press of a button, they are not entirely satisfied. Without human warmth, without someone to talk to, people can't be fully human. The self unrecognized by another is only half a self. Particularly in Japan, the self becomes half dead if it is not blended with others.

Just how high a price will we pay if our jobs are filled by microcomputers and human connections are cut off between people? The warning is the vending-machine anecdote. The less opportunity a person has to respond and communicate emotionally, the greater the ultimate harm to the self.

Vertical Relationships

The hermit crab perishes when it is pulled from its shell. Similarly, when torn from his "shell," a human being cannot survive without great damage to his personality and his ability to cope with life. The "shell" of human life is the social group. Alienation and isolation from society are a fatal blow. No human being can survive without support from the members of his social group.

This was especially important in Japan's early centuries, in a rice-producing society. The people needed mutual help badly to accomplish their work. Accordingly, the Japanese came to emphasize loyalty to the group as a means of surviving. This loyalty of members toward the group is an eloquent testimony to the cohesiveness of Japanese social groups. The question between members, "How long have you eaten your rice in the group?" indicates the strong belief in a hierarchy defined by seniority, with only minor regard for actual performance. The importance of the hierarchy in Japan is hard for most foreigners to understand and accept. Also, relations between groups are extremely cold. Members of other groups are always "others," and both emotionally and intellectually the Japanese are unprepared to deal with others in a horizontal relationship. This is, of course, the nature of a vertical society.

Now I would like to deal with the individual personality in this sort of society—how it is delimited, how it reaches out to others. The vertical society has had a major impact on the "self" of the Japanese people.

A few years ago, I visited the Tohoku region. I was taken around by a friend, a cheerful, energetic young man who talked pleasantly about his own work, the history of the region, and many other subjects. Though it was one of the warmest days in summer, both of us enjoyed ourselves tremendously for over two hours. Then we visited his place of work. At lunch, arranged for me through the kindness of his supervisor, I was surprised to see his attitude change dramatically. He utterly lost his previous cheerfulness and energy, and his spirit seemed to be drained. Everything about my young host—and his co-workers, I might add—became formal and stiff in the presence of the supervisor, even the way he opened his mouth and chewed his food. The restrained attitude of all these young men was due in part to the formality of the occasion, to the fact that their superior had gone to the trouble of arranging lunch for a visitor and had invited them to join in. But it was also due to an ethical rule of Japanese society. In a group, each member is expected to minimize his individual presence and be as self-effacing as possible. Acting as if one were afraid of one's supervisor is a manifestation of the group convention of absolute self-effacement.

This is not a special feature of the Tohoku region, but is true throughout Japan. Within any organization, the role assigned to a person by the group always takes precedence over his personal desires. The individual self, its motives and attitudes, should therefore be suppressed. For this reason, some people say that it is impossible for them to express themselves in a group setting; others, in response to the same situation, insist that what is important is *how* one expresses oneself. It all comes down to the kind of work philosophy one adopts. The young man who guided me around the Tohoku region had selected the former approach, and as a result, when he entered the group his personality was suppressed. For all practical purposes, it was dissolved.

Social groups in Japan also demand an extreme degree of loyalty and uniformity. In the rigid order of the rank-conscious society, defined by the seniority system, people are compelled to put on their masks and, from within the confines of "humility" and "politeness," demonstrate their abilities as inconspicuously as possible. The success of modern "Japanese management," so widely admired in the world today, lies in forming groups for production and making these groups the object of loyalty and service. The relation between employer and employee is no different from that between feudal lord and subject, and lifetime employment is based on the feudal idea that no man should serve two lords.

The seniority system, which rewards people not simply for ability or effort but chiefly for length of stay, seems to have satisfied the superficial need for equality of Japanese workers. Thus Japanese management has been able to secure and retain the loyal service of its workers in a way that is envied by the West. Also, by giving workers the security of lifetime employment and the benefits that accrue more or less automatically through the seniority system, Japanese industry has been able to pacify the unions and work out a cooperative relationship with them.

This lord-subject relationship is unlike the contractual relationship between employer and employee in the West. It is based on the feudal concept of *on*—a blessing or favor handed down, not only by an invisible being, but also by a social or political superior. *On* carries with it the obligation on the part of the recipient to return something for that blessing or favor. In the West a contract can be fulfilled by the equalizing of wages and labor. But the social obligation incurred by *on* can never be completely repaid. *On* is, in other words, the spirit that impelled feudal subjects to defend the castle of their lord to the last man; and this spirit, in modified form, lives on in the modern samurai worker, making the company he devotes himself to tremendously competitive in the marketplace. *On* is the psychological shaft-to-wheel relationship between management and labor. The vertical society still operates in Tokugawa style.

Two Supervisors

At dawn on February 26, 1936, the young officers of the infantry surrounded the snow-covered Prime Minister's residence, and shook the Japanese to the core with their bloody coup d'état. A memorial recording of parts of that incident was released by NHK (Japan Broadcasting Association) and was televised nation-wide on February 26, 1979, on a program called "The Secret Record of the 2/26 Incident." The voices of those who participated in the coup d'état 43 years earlier were so alive that audiences felt as if they were really involved. The segment that struck me the most was a telephone conversation between a Sergeant Uemura and his previous commanding officer, Lieutenant Takahashi. In the conversation Takahashi urged Uemura, who had joined the rebel party, to abandon the rebel cause. Even though the appeal came from his former commanding officer, Uemura appeared unmoved. In response to Takahashi's plea, "You have a pistol, don't you? Kill your commanding officer and come back to us," Uemura replied, "It's too late now." Takahashi argued, "Any soldier who takes up arms against the Emperor is not a Japanese soldier. You don't have any duty to obey the rebels' orders." Still Uemura showed no indication of compliance. Finally, Takahashi asked, "Don't you value your life?" To which Uemura replied, "No, I don't."

Anyone familiar with the prewar Japanese army would real-ize immediately that Takahashi's appeal could have little effect. The prewar army had an established hierarchy, perhaps the strictest in the world, which required absolute obedience to the orders of the commanding officer. Thus Uemura and the other rebel soldiers were constrained to follow their present com-manders, not their previous ones. There was no escape from this dictum. Even when the Emperor ordered the rebels to return to the main force, the soldiers could not move. They had been educated only to follow orders. Rebel or desert—they were caught between the Emperor's order and the strict iron rule of the army. It was not a matter of personal choice—so firm and thorough was their indoctrination that they could not even consider switching loyalties. The commanding officer's orders were their sole standard for action. The question of right or wrong never entered the picture.

In the end, the rebel forces did obey the Emperor's order, and the responsible officers were arrested. The lower officers and soldiers returned to their original force. Following that, Uemura was expelled from the army and stripped of his rank. In all this, even up to the loss of his military rank, Sergeant Uemura always followed his superior's orders, the implicit orders of the Japanese Imperial Army. In all his actions, no "self" was discernible at all; in fact, it was self-effacement. Still, service to the rebel forces was not recognized as loyal service to the army, so he lost his rank and military status. Did Uemura resent this refusal to recognize that he "was only following orders"? Probably not. More likely, he chalked it up to fate and resigned himself to his miserable luck. I should make it clear here, however, that such an army no longer exists in Japan.

Now let me describe an incident which demonstrates the exact opposite attitude to "following orders." It took place among the American occupation forces in Japan after World War II. Just beyond the turning point of the Fukuoka International Marathon Course, in northern Kyushu Island, there are traces of the old Hakata Naval Air Base. A bit further on, in Saitozaki, an Air Force squadron in charge of the Shikanoshima Radar Site was stationed. (At present both the radar and the base are, of course, gone.) One day, officers at the base discovered that some very important military equipment was missing. Presuming it was a theft from outside the base, the commanding officer ordered the commissioned officers and soldiers to search all the houses in Saitozaki, which then had roughly 2,000 families. The officers and soldiers were rather excited by the event and poured down on the village, rummaging through every house for the missing equipment with a fine-tooth comb. It was clear from their attitude that they were as interested in what made up a Japanese house as they were in finding the missing equipment. This was clearly not a case of "absolute obedience to orders."

The most interesting thing was that two officers refused to follow orders and locked themselves up in the officers' quarters. Strictly speaking, in an army, we may call this insubordination. When asked the reason for their resistance, they replied, "This order goes against the principles of American democracy. Whether we are the occupation forces or not, the war is over. Therefore, we refuse to comply." The incident taught me just how highly the Americans regard the self and how respect for the self is intimately related to the development of American democracy.

Returning to our former topic: After Sergeant Uemura was stripped of his rank and driven out of the armed forces, he fled to Manchuria and became a police officer. (In prewar Japan, military or military-related personnel who made some blunder or fell from favor were often sent to Manchuria.) After several years, Lieutenant Takahashi also went to Manchuria and visited his previous subordinate, Uemura. Of course, we have no way of knowing what they said to each other or how they rekindled old memories, but this certainly stands as an example of the way the relationship between Japanese officers and their men continues forever.

Sergeant Uemura joined the rebel forces by the order of his commander, but at the same time he was strongly urged to remain loyal to the main force by his former commander. Uemura listened to Takahashi's plea with all the deference that a subordinate should accord to his superior. But it had already reached the point of being "too late," and despite Takahashi's informal order, Uemura was obliged to follow the direct orders of his commander at the time. Thus it is apparent that he had two bosses.

In like manner, most Japanese have two or more supervisors (direct and indirect) within the same organization. Everyone has a boss immediately above him, who has direct control over him; at the same time, an employee retains a strong tie with his previous supervisors and feels that he is still subordinate to them and must listen to and accept their advice. This is a hallmark of Japanese industrial society. Even new members of the company, if they have gotten a job through some high-ranking inside connection, will have a special feeling for the insider, regarding him as different from other department or division heads. Also, those who enter without connections will try to find a "second boss" from among their superiors and more often than not will develop their careers utilizing such a tie.

These "second bosses" are not, of course, officially recognized, but there is a general awareness of such relationships among the members of the company. Perhaps we should call the direct supervisor the "formal boss" and the indirect supervisor, whoever he may be, the "informal boss." Depending upon the nature of the particular company, and the prevailing working conditions, one or the other may have a stronger impact on any individual company member.

If I may add one further note: In the West a "boss" is the person who is directly above you in the organization and supervises your work. However, in Japan everyone above you in the pyramidal structure is called your *jōshi* (superior). Not every *jōshi* has real supervisory power, but the *jōshi* usually pride themselves on at least occasionally taking a supervisory position. This phenomenon shows just how easy it is for a worker to have two or more supervisors in an organization and how all members of the higher echelons of the company play a supervisory role for all those below them.

The desire to attach oneself to two or more supervisors is a result of the vertical nature of the Japanese organization, in which commitment and loyalty take precedence over ability. Since everything is done by teamwork and individual ability and performance cannot logically be used as a means of determining promotion, the competition for vertical advancement can have its seamy side. The channels of advancement and success are more readily available to those who have the favors of *jōshi*. Even after retirement, the close relationship between former superior and former subordinate usually continues. This is one of the dividends of the vertical society. By the same token, having two or more supervisors in one organization further delimits the self. In precisely the same way that a young wife suffers under the domination of both her husband and her mother-in-law, the worker in an organization often finds himself in a desperate position. The fate of Sergeant Uemura illustrates the suffering this kind of dual allegiance can produce. In order to succeed and move upward in the group, a person must be thoroughly experienced in such matters.

Each and every one of us is part of a group, and we sustain ourselves by virtue of our relationship with that group. In Japan, however, it is a matter not simply of being included in the group but of being "blended" into it. It is a custom in Japanese society that the individual should bend his back, hunch his shoulders, and efface himself as much as possible—as the language of politeness *(keigo)* and the bowing act represent. Egoism, or self-regard, is the most despised characteristic within a group. It is a cause for exclusion from the group and can lead to the destruction of a person's social credibility. Yet there is no one who is without egoism entirely. Knowing how to control this egoism, and when and to what extent to demonstrate it, is the essential skill for living within the group. It is comparatively more difficult to exercise egoism in Japan than in the West.

The Tortoise and the Hare

There isn't a single man, woman, or child in Japan who is not familiar with the nursery tale of the tortoise and the hare. From the first moment of awareness, every child hears his mother singing the ditty about the race between these two fabled creatures, and the tortoise's ultimate victory. Drummed into him from earliest childhood, the story and the moral it conveys become an essential part of the child's personality. What is the spirit of this children's story?

The hare, speedy and gifted as a racer, lost because he was lazy and took a nap on the way to the goal; and the tortoise, slow fellow that he was, triumphed by his persistence. "Diligence is the key!"—that is the samurai spirit and the moral this tale inculcates in every Japanese child.

The explosive modernization program instituted by the Meiji government in an effort to catch up with the West and the subsequent industrial development and militarism Japan experienced were all based on this mythic determination. The so-called "samurai employee" and the "samurai company president" (complimentary terms for hard workers) grew up listening to this nursery story about the hare and the tortoise.

Persistence is very important, and unless people put their full energies into an enterprise, be it government or industry, they have little chance of succeeding. But there is a great danger of misunderstanding inherent in this fable and its moral, "Slow and steady wins the race." The danger is the tendency to regard ability and performance as secondary assets. The idea that even a tortoise can win a foot race, if it is really determined to do so, supports the belief common among the Japanese that perseverance is more important than talent. During World War II this brave samurai spirit moved people to face the enemy machine guns with blunderbusses, and to charge with bamboo spears against bazooka fire. These examples illustrate a total disregard for ability that had tragic consequences.

It was indeed fortunate for our slow friend the tortoise that the hare relaxed his mind and took a nap. If he hadn't, there would have been no contest. The present "examination hell" that holds all young people in Japan in its thrall is another example of this disregard for differences in ability. Everyone is urged to climb up the hierarchical ladder—regardless of his native abilities, or conspicuous lack of them— and is egged on with the familiar Japanese admonition, *"Ganbatte!"* ("Try hard!") Though there are often calls for reform, as long as the Japanese are mesmerized by the fable of the tortoise and the hare, any effort at reform is doomed to fail.

As previously noted, Japanese society judges a person's worth by his title, in rather simple-minded fashion. It gives highest value to those toward the top of the social pyramid. There is only one value system, and it is monolithic. Therefore, it is essential to have some sort of certification of quality at an early point in the hierarchical climb. This first (and very often last) testament of ability is the academic record, which is the credential every student needs to join the industrial force. It is the student's first important title to show to society. In order to gain this title, young people must desperately pour their energies into study for the university entrance examination. They have very little chance to reflect on their innate abilities, very little time to consider other directions.

Since the Japanese are a homogeneous people, perhaps there is little reason to expect great differences in ability among them. But even though they may be physically similar, each has a different nature and different abilities. A hare is bound to win a land race, but it would be another story in the water. In the same way, depending on how the world turns and the task we put ourselves to, our abilities will produce very different results. Many people in Japan do secretly seem to believe they might have done better if they had focused their energies in another direction. But with the monolithic value system, everyone throws himself into the fray for vertical promotion with little heed to his innate abilities. If the Japanese were more self-minded on the upward social climb and found more time to reflect properly on their talents and aptitudes, they might pursue goals more in consonance with their true abilities and values. When and if this happens, Japan will make further progress.

Horizontal Terror

Not everyone can rise to the top. When you build a castle wall, you need little stones as well as big rocks. Every society has a need for plodders as well as geniuses, for those with no more than an elementary school education as well as for university graduates. Nevertheless, in Japan vertical promotion is so highly valued, and the competition for it so fierce, that no one is content staying where he is. Those who remain at the lower levels of the hierarchy are known as "the goods at the bottom of the pile."

Since everyone theoretically has an equal opportunity for advancement, those who fail to reach the upper levels are regarded as the losers or the defeated in life and bear a heavy psychological burden. In a country with distinct class divisions, people seem to be satisfied within the confines of their own class—a bus driver is content among bus drivers, an engineer among engineers. Not so in Japan. Everyone can and does jump into the climb.

Therefore, in a vertical society, every co-worker is a rival. All those related to you horizontally—that is, all your peers—are a threat. The expression "to have your legs pulled out from under you" suggests that the pulling comes from below, but in most cases it's a shove from the side—by a colleague or a co-worker at approximately the same level who has the same aspirations that you do. The Japanese expression *yokoyari* (an interruption; literally, "side spearing") describes the nature of the threat posed by colleagues. The Japanese practice of circulating a buck slip (*ringisho*) as a way of preparing the groundwork for a consensus shows just how important it is to prevent *yokoyari*, or sidetracking of your effort to make a decision and build a consensus.

Competition between groups follows the same pattern. The most dangerous enemy is the company that produces the same product. Publishing houses are in fierce competition with other publishers, newspapers with newspapers, universities with universities, town with town, and, unfortunately, government ministry with government ministry.

This rivalry stirs up a spirit of enthusiasm that encourages development and increases production. Thus, as long as it is not excessive, it is a healthy phenomenon. But excessive rivalry causes friction, and friction can have exactly the opposite results.

The Japanese are perhaps the coldest people in the world to those they consider outsiders—people who are not part of their group. Everyone in Japan has seen or experienced the following scene: A tired-looking commuter relinquishes his seat to someone on the train. Listening to their conversation, one invariably discovers that they are friends or members of the same group. In most cases, a lower-ranking employee offers his seat to a higher-ranking employee. But the same person who so readily and cheerfully gave up his seat to an "insider" would push aside an "outsider" in a mad dash for that seat. There are bus drivers and railway employees who cannot reply to commuters in a civil manner. They are so cold and just plain rude that commuters would be better off trying to talk to a vending machine. Owing to the nature of the vertical society, the Japanese do not feel the need to show any feeling or regard for "outsiders." They still live inside their fief.

The problem becomes even more severe when the Japanese are abroad. The coldness, the actual belligerence, that two unknown samurai direct to each other in their stony glances when they meet is startling. Yet it is a behavior that they can't seem to escape. Can we explain this coldness simply as lack of sociability? Chie Nakane, in *Human Relations in a Vertical Society* (written in Japanese), offers this interpretation: "The uncertainty of someone unaccustomed to dealing with equals becomes mixed up with the surprise of suddenly meeting someone in an alien environment. The belligerent behavior is produced to cover up that weakness." The most important phrase in Dr. Nakane's interpretation is "someone unaccustomed to dealing with equals," or, more precisely, with equals outside one's group.

Feelings or obligations are hardly recognized beyond the perimeter of the group. It is not just the bus drivers and station employees who feel no obligation to be civil to those outside their circle. The passengers feel no need to be especially polite and sociable either. This rather dry relationship is the norm among people who are unrelated by group membership. It is undoubtedly a carryover from the Tokugawa period, when people were not used to dealing with "equals" from a different fief.

Giri and Ninjō

In contrast to the above, the Japanese show the utmost devotion to those inside their group. Every member of a group is bound by ties of *giri* (interrelated social duty) and *ninjō* (human feeling). *Giri* is the creation of kinshiplike ties between people; it is a relationship of interdependence brought about by *on* (a favor, or debt of gratitude as a result of receiving a favor). It is, according to the dictionary, also the proper moral duty of all Japanese.

The fundamental group unit in Japan is the family. All other groups mimic the family and incorporate its cohesion, exclusiveness, and hierarchical structure. These groups also take on a psychological version of the "blood ties" that unite a family. All institutions—factories, schools, and others—extend these psychological blood ties over their members, binding them together, helping them, relating them to each other, and finally, delimiting them. All these relationships take on kinshiplike *ninjō* (human feeling) along with *giri*. At times this feeling for other people gets out of hand and becomes meddling in the affairs of others. Then the "ties of *giri* and *ninjō*" sometimes become a burden that weighs doubly on the individual.

However, a nationwide survey in 1981 showed that 69

percent of the Japanese people still considered *giri* and *ninjō* the most important factors in human relations, while 22 percent held "personal creed and belief" to be more important. The remaining 9 percent had no opinion. *Giri-ninjō* is an unwritten law which ensures the harmonious functioning of individuals in a group. It is sort of social contract modeled after the family.

In the West, contracts are often used to prevent interference between individuals, but in Japan *giri-ninjō* acts as the link between the self and others, a concept entirely appropriate to a homogeneous people organized along family lines. *Giri-ninjō* is the "natural contract" that the Japanese have lived by for centuries. The rules have never been committed to writing. To this day, few companies bind their employees with written contracts. The words and actions of employees are governed less by written regulations than by *giri-ninjō,* which each takes as his unspoken guide. For this reason I would like to describe Japan as the "*on*-tract" society—in contrast to the "contract" society of the West. People are governed by the spirit of *on,* the sense of social obligation which usually interrelates *giri* and *ninjō*.

For example, according to company rules and regulations, every worker has the right to take a certain number of paid vacation days. But if a certain worker were to use up all his allotted days for his own pleasure, he would acquire an unfavorable reputation in the company. Those who use up their entire paid leave, without considering that their fellow workers are still busily at work, come to be known as ingrates. *Giri-ninjō* governs the workers more than the formal rules and regulations of the company.

In contrast, when dealing with outsiders, the Japanese will apply contracts and regulations with a cold efficiency. Even so, if a familiarity gradually develops between the two parties, *giri-ninjō* will begin to replace contractual arrangements. For example, once a relationship has been established, there may no longer be a need for a formal contract between an author and his publisher. Or, as often happens in Japan, a contract may be canceled when both parties feel they can ignore the rules and defer to *giri-ninjō* in certain decisions. The nonlogical society has operated for hundreds of years by these principles. Even today, *giri-ninjō* guides and binds the Japanese with great strength.

Giri-ninjō also influences Japan's economic sector. The main reason for the present trade imbalance between Japan and the West is that it is extremely difficult for foreign traders to gain a foothold in the Japanese market, especially in the distribution sector. As pointed out earlier, exclusivity is a characteristic of all Japanese society, but wholesale distributors are even more exclusive than most Japanese groups. If you are an unknown face, you have almost no chance of finding a way in, no matter how long you talk about prices and goods. The distributors have this attitude toward other Japanese as well. If other traders try to enter their territory "from the side," there will be a long and bitter battle. Totally rejecting and repelling outsiders—whether from another country or another "fief"—is an old trait inherited from the *mura* (enclosed village society), where it was the main means of self-defense. Even today, if you enter a farming village, you will feel the full force of this utter exclusivity in operation.

The distribution sector of the economy is not unlike the farming village—it is the symbolic village of the enclosed merchant class. The merchants' cold rejection of those who try to cut in from the side (that is, as equal but unknown outsiders) is the often discussed "non-tariff barrier." Any independent operator who tries to enter another group from the side will run smack into this non-tariff barrier. Such a person must be sure to carry along a letter of introduction from a *kao-yaku* (person with social influence), or have a "fixer" arrange the meeting for him. Without this form of *giri-ninjō*, the effort is almost sure to end in failure, or at best to take an unbelievably long time. For this reason, the distribution sector in Japan is extremely inefficient compared with the highly efficient production sector.

Figure 4 summarizes the trade picture between Japan and

Figure 4. Exports between Japan and the West.

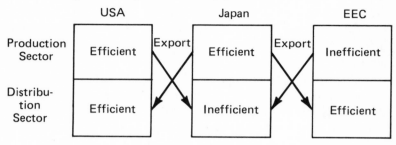

the USA and between Japan and the European Economic Community (EEC). As the arrows show, exports from America or the EEC have to make inroads into the inefficient distribution sector of Japan, while the efficient production sector of Japan is connected with the efficient distributors in the USA and the EEC. The consequences for the balance of trade are obvious.

The Double-Structured Self

Primitive societies lacked organized means of transportation and depended mainly on cattle and horses. Because mobility was so restricted, the largest groups they could form were limited to a few hundred, all related by blood ties. We can imagine that in such kinship groups individual egoism was a near impossibility and probably did not exist. Survival in primitive society depended on absolute loyalty to the group, a concept that was no doubt encouraged and strengthened by the society's leaders. While loyalty within the group was emphasized, animosity toward all other groups was the rule. This anti-outsider sentiment may have been the first sort of egoism—a group egoism, to be sure, but egoism nonetheless.

As society progressed and spread and the blood ties weakened, individual egoism began to develop. In the West individuals were permitted to express themselves within the group, and contracts and rules were developed to control this social interaction and to prevent conflict among various individual egos. In contrast, in Japan conflict was avoided by the abandonment of individualism and the dissolution of the self into the group—that is, the encouragement of *wa,* or harmonious concord. Social progress was achieved through the ties of the group. Nevertheless, group-consciousness can never completely eliminate the individual ego. The primeval group egoism and the individual egoism that came after it exist together even in Japan. Each individual ego is at times under the sway of the group ego, and at other times acts on its own commands. Thus each self has a double nature, a two-layered structure. The one is *tatemae* (public front) and the other *honne* (private intention).

In most cases, the group ego and the individual ego run along the same track. Problems arise when a person tries to fulfill his private desires under the guise of the group will. This we may call "the double structure of the self" which is partly exposed in the "group-directed individualism" described in Chapter 1. Let us continue investigating this double nature with some examples.

Tatemae (Public Front) and Honne (Private Intention)

These days there is little greenery left in the urban areas of Japan. Citizens all over the nation are interested in improving the situation and making their towns better places to live. But when election season comes around, this interest seems to vanish: the towns are transformed overnight into gigantic billboards, with posters plastered on walls, electric poles, bus stops, and train schedules, and with handbills scattered here and there. Yet if we listen to the speeches of the candidates represented in these posters and handbills, they're all the same: "I want to devote myself to righting the wrongs of our world. I want to make our town a better place to live." They are, on the contrary, industriously uglifying the town with their promotional literature; and their ceaseless loudspeaker announcements beaming from sound trucks make it nearly impossible for people to live in peace.

There is nothing wrong with the personal ambition of a Diet candidate who wants to be elected—if his personal desire is consonant with his professed concern for the group will—in this case, making the town beautiful. The problem arises when personal ambition is so strong that it pays no heed to group desires and instead pastes posters all over town and makes the city an ugly, unpleasant place. In this case, the candidate is exploiting the group will for personal ends, hiding behind the skirts of the public. If the candidate were sincere about beautifying the town, he would not put up posters so indiscriminately. This is an example of the double self I am referring to. It is not unlike certain souvenir foods that people buy at tourist spots: from the outside, the food container looks quite large—the public front; but upon closer inspection, it has a very shallow false bottom—the private ambition. The point is that people know of its falseness but buy it anyway and give it to a neighbor or a friend. The people approve the double standard.

This double self, which pretends to work for the group and hides a real intention to serve its own ends, is a worldwide phenomenon. It is the oldest trick of politicians, everywhere and at all times. But in some countries public figures are more fastidious about covering up such behavior, because they know if they are caught red-handed their career is over. In Japan, however, such two-facedness is rather an accepted practice: personal ambition *(honne)* is typically hidden beneath the guise of group interests *(tatemae)*. The citizens pretend not to notice the conflict of interests, much like the citizens pressed down by the samurai class in the Tokugawa era. So traditionally rooted is this practice that the public feels it is impossible to insist upon rectification. The Japanese seem to be resigned to the double standard.

Company Consciousness and Work Consciousness

It is often remarked that workers in the West, particularly in America, are dedicated to their work, while workers in Japan are dedicated to their companies. There is a difference between a "work consciousness" and a "company consciousness."

In the prewar society of Japan, everyone devoted himself to his country, and self-sacrifice was the ideal governing the nation. With the defeat of Japan in World War II, that nationalism was destroyed and the Japanese were thrown into a spiritual vacuum. A naive opportunism became the guiding principle in a land where no one had ever had the experience of simply serving himself and enjoying personal freedom. The people were somewhat at a loss and looked for a new spiritual basis for joining together. A "group opportunism" was forged, and all energies were poured into the company organization—the people's economic reliance.

In this reorientation from nationalism to "companyism," the group orientation of the Japanese experienced a renaissance. If you look into the giant conglomerates like Mitsui, Mitsubishi, Sumitomo, and the National Railway, the "company is the family" concept existed years before the war. But this budding companyism had to surrender to nationalism during the war. All the families were unified in devoting themselves to their nation. After the country was defeated, nationalism diminished and "companyism" came on the scene with renewed vigor. Though in the larger society the company is only a private organization, for those who work there it is a society in toto, a public institution. The notion of "public" has always been little appreciated in Japan, and it has been easy for a worker to mistake his private place of employment for his only "public."

In the West, some workers do regard their place of work as their sole means of sustenance, but this sustenance often carries no more than an economic meaning. Beyond that, these workers have little interest in the workplace. In Japan, the workplace has become the repository of the workers' hearts and souls, a source of total sustenance; as a result, the company has come to be regarded as the equivalent of a feudal fief. *Shokuba* (workplace) in Japan has quite a different connotation from "workplace" in the West.

Very few people deny that the unimpeded, all-embracing company-consciousness rooted in "industrial feudalism" was the main support of the Japanese economy in the postwar development period. The cultural force that contributed to strengthening this consciousness has built three pillars of Japanese management: lifetime employment (cohesiveness), the seniority system (hierarchy), and the in-company union (exclusivism). These will be discussed in Chapter 4.

Now in order for a company to be continuously accepted by the workers and to encourage them to devote their whole life to it, the company must provide the dependability and objectivity of a public institution. When the company starts cutting corners and eliminates its middle-aged and older workers, retaining the younger ones because their lower wages make them more economical, an economic ideal may be realized, but the company loses any claim it might have on workers' loyalty and trust. Then company-consciousness weakens among employees.

The relationship between labor and management today may be as close as it was in the past, but it has changed a little. Loyalty to the company has weakened, and in its place a new self-defense mechanism is operating. The recent self-development boom in Japan is evidence of just this. Since there seems little possibility of ever returning to the national self-sacrifice theme of the prewar years, the company must find some way to keep company-consciousness from becoming another relic of the past. With the slogan "new organization man," management hopes to rekindle an awareness of and pride in the company. At present, the retreating specter of the "company mentality" and the sprouting of professional pride combine to create the self of the Japanese worker. There is obviously a contradiction here. The company mentality is a manifestation of the group ego, but the new professional pride is an individual phenomenon. Traditionally accustomed to contradictory practices, the Japanese worker resolves this contradiction by earnestly displaying the company mentality outwardly while burning with a new professional pride inside.

Since workers are forced to retire between ages 55 and 60, it is impossible to block this new self-awareness. Today many workers are considering other alternatives, such as another job if need be or other work following retirement. So, while one part of the Japanese self is devoting its energies to the group, another part is preparing for advancement outside the confines of the group. The company may try to "cure" these employees, but any on-the-job education programs will have a limited effect as long as the conditions which create the double self remain.

Thus the number of people who are able to satisfy their own desires under the aegis of the group—that is, those who are skilled in manipulating the double self—is increasing by leaps and bounds. The group logic that employers try to use as a motivator has actually become a protective umbrella for these people. The company's name printed on their calling cards still serves to establish their social status, but in a way their behavior is now inner-directed, aiming at self-satisfaction.

Work Machine and Consumption Machine

Blessed with an enriched education and the benefits of a modern communications network, young people today are not naive. They are remarkably canny when it comes to seeing through the pretenses of their own society. However, they lack the strength of mind to try to reform that society. Instead, their interests lie in living a pleasant and comfortable life. The adventure of reform is not for them. Because of these changes, a new kind of "workaholic" is in the making. In order to acquire the goods and services that make their lives pleasant and comfortable, these young people are willing to work very hard, and even to appear to bend their wills to the group mentality. But actually they are bitter and frustrated workaholics. Their work is nothing but a necessary evil. They find no satisfaction in it. In order to vent the frustration they feel at work, they buy more and more of the goods and services that give them satisfaction and take their minds away from the job. It becomes a vicious circle. Their desperate effort to restore the self that is being sacrificed at work leads them to indulge themselves senselessly when they are off the job.

These young people are doubly exploited—as "work machines" on their jobs, and as "consumption machines" for industry. They are both workaholics and funaholics, if I may coin a phrase. They are reduced to the robotic functions of producing and consuming. "To find satisfaction through your hobbies and leisure pursuits" sounds very modern and elevated, but it also suggests that one is not getting satisfaction in one's work. If the only reason people work is to indulge themselves, their interest in their jobs falls to the level of simply earning money. The states of *wabi* and *sabi* discussed previously can be reached only through self-development of the highest degree, which presupposes a maturity of character not evident in simple sensual indulgence. A one-sided emphasis on fun, to the exclusion of work, is not the way to *wabi* and *sabi*. As a result of this new attitude, the samurai workers are deteriorating a bit.

The tendency to have more interest in one's after-hours activities than in one's work is evident even in Japan's Self-Defense Forces. According to a published survey carried out by the Officers' Corps, "The officer class is very patriotic and regards the army as its life. Most of the young soldiers, however, are more interested in their own activities—in enjoying their personal interests."

Group Logic and Individual Desire

Any organization is more than the sum total of the individuals in it. The relationships between those individuals are just as much a part of the organization as a whole. The problem lies in adjusting and harmonizing these relationships. The necessity of controlling relationships creates a hierarchical order within the group. Certain people are placed above others, and power tends to be concentrated in the upper strata. This is the way in which power and authority develop. Finally, authority becomes a self-existing element, quite separate from those who created it.

In Japanese groups, authority quickly takes on this autonomous nature, which makes it extremely difficult, if not impossible, for people to express their personal wishes or desires. Thus to the degree that the Japanese participate in a group, they are forced to set aside their own personality (suppress personal egoism) and identify with the group personality (support group egoism). This is what produces the double personality of the Japanese worker.

The double personality is evident in incidents where a normally "good" person commits illegitimate acts in the name of the group. For example, an otherwise decent, law-abiding citizen covers up the pollution created by his company and commits other improper acts for the sake of the group. Such a citizen is responding to the group ideal—unquestioned obedience to the leader. When the public self that has pledged allegiance to the ideals of the group becomes melded with the private self, the individual can perform unthinkable acts with no apparent damage to his conscience.

Individual integrity would demand testifying truthfully in accordance with one's oath. But when private desire ("I want to see my way out of this mess, even if I have to lie") and public logic ("It's for the company's sake, so I needn't worry my conscience") combine, people easily abandon their integrity and lie boldly without remorse. Here we have the double structure of group logic and private desire. Because group logic overrides conscience, it is easy for people to escape the discomfort that might otherwise accompany such patently self-serving acts. Someone who is "sacrificing" his conscience in order to uphold the group's ideals suffers no pangs of remorse.

There are people whose conscience does bother them occasionally. And suicide is often the result when the private self fails to meld successfully with the logic of the group. This is the last escape for a self besieged on all sides. Many times those involved in scandal and corruption, unable to resolve the contradiction between their private conscience and the will of the group, commit suicide in desperation. They become sandwiched mercilessly between these conflicting demands and see no other way out.

This phenomenon is not so common in the West. When the logic of the group conflicts with private conscience, the individual is likely to rebel and betray the group. Examples are the in-company accusation against the pollution created by the company and the testimony of some of the high officials implicated in the Watergate scandal. It seems very difficult for an individual in the West to act against his own conscience and follow group orders without considerable anguish. Even if he eventually complies under duress, his conscience may not leave him alone.

What follows is neither a scandal nor an anecdote about government officials. It is the story of Everett Alvarez, the Navy lieutenant commander who was the first American prisoner of war in Vietnam. Alvarez was taken prisoner after President Johnson ordered the bombing attack on North Vietnam. All through his long internment he never came to doubt the rightness of the Vietnam War. He was taken quite by surprise, however, when he returned home following his release on February 12, 1973. This model soldier received a shock that he hardly deserved—and it came from his own family. His wife had divorced him in his absence in 1970; she had remarried and already had a child by her new husband. His sister had joined the antiwar movement, and had participated in a demonstration at the White House. Even his mother had announced through the mass media that she thought Nixon had tricked the public and that she was against the war.

The members of Commander Alvarez's family were led to do what they did by the belief that private conscience takes precedence over group logic. Whatever self-interest they might have had, they did not disguise it under the cloak of group will. Each had a personal commitment that led her to oppose the group, follow her own conscience, and, eventually, reject the deeds of her own husband, brother, or son.

The principle illustrated by this relatively well-known story is not exceptional, and the degree of respect for individual reasoning and belief it demonstrates is by no means unusual in the West. In the individualist countries, society exists to protect the rights and interests of the individual. There is little need to create a double self to satisfy the needs of the group. But in Japan individuals form groups to survive. They agree to live under the group mandate that they create together, and they cherish the rules that govern the group. When individual belief is in opposition to group belief, pressure is put on the individual to conform. A good deal of juggling of personal and group considerations goes on behind the scenes, and the double self emerges in an attempt to satisfy both sets of interests.

3

HUSBAND AND WIFE
IN TRADITIONAL SOCIETY

Some years ago a young historian told me about a strange system of marriage in a remote hinterland of a certain Asian country. In this isolated community, when a boy reaches adulthood, he marries several women and owns them in common with his brothers. Sometimes three brothers have two wives, or even five wives, in common. A man is allowed socially to own any number of wives as long as he can support them. By the same token, women have several husbands in common. If an agreement is reached, someone's wife can be passed over to another family. Accordingly, a child may have two or more fathers, since the mother can never be sure which husband is the father of that child. Nevertheless, the historian said, no trouble has ever occurred, because the inhabitants of the area have taken the system for granted for many years.

There is only one restriction. A man never can marry a woman (or take over someone's wife) from the same village, regardless of how charming she is or how much he pays for her. A matrimonial union within the same village is strictly prohibited. This is the absolute code of the area. Furthermore, a newly married woman who has come from a neighboring village must return to her native village once after the wedding ceremony and share a bed with a man there.

Under this traditional code of life, the people have passed quite peacefully and happily from generation to generation and have had no conflict whatsoever.

This is a far cry from the random sexual mating or free sex which we sometimes find in modern civilized society. The traditions and customs of a people always have some deeply rooted significance. The polygamous custom of the community described above was the people's way of meeting their isolated geographical conditions. If they had had a monogamous system, as we do, with family members branching off at every marriage, their home economy would have been split into pieces. The dividing of livestock and land would have caused domestic conflict among brothers and sisters, and the confusion would have made it easy for other tribes to invade the area. The people chose polygamous marriage as the best way to unify all the villages and maintain their peaceful community. The prohibition against marriage within the same village was no doubt designed to prevent the hereditary infelicity which often results from intermarriage. The custom of having a newly married woman share a bed with a man from her native village was probably established to maintain friendly relations with the neighboring village. All are part of the best system for these people, as polished by wisdom.

The culture of any country is the sum total of its values. Every race has cultivated its own culture through its long history and has created the most suitable lifestyle for itself. Therefore, every culture, without exception, is unique. Polygamy might easily seem a strange custom or a primitive practice to Westerners, but from the viewpoint of the villagers described above, the monogamous custom of modern civilized societies would seem unnatural.

The Japanese too have marital customs that may seem

unusual to people of other nations. The concept of marriage in Japan is different from that in the West. The most distinctive feature is probably the arranged marriage, which has been practiced in Japan for centuries. During the Turbulent Age (1467–1575) and the following transitional stage and Tokugawa period (1603–1867), *daimyō* and samurai were all very eager for power. A daughter could, through her marriage, strengthen the family's relation with another family, as was true in the feudal age in the West. A girl was therefore raised carefully, for she was a very valuable item in interfamily politics. A marriage was arranged to suit the family's needs. Since the marriage was not the result of attraction between the young couple, conjugal love was a secondary development, to be achieved later by the pair. In this system, the sexual fidelity of the couple was considered most important, as it played a role in keeping the family unit together. For this reason, many private studies on age differences, physical flexibility, and development of sexual competence were conducted during the Tokugawa period to determine sexual compatibility.

Arranged Marriage

The arranged marriage existed in its full form throughout the Tokugawa period. It is therefore not surprising that the attitudes and customs derived from the system remain in the modern industrial society of Japan. For example, young elites—samurai who seemingly have the greatest social prospects—go about searching for a mate of brilliant social standing. These young elites are the "promising" bachelors of large business companies and bachelors of the "career group" in the central government bureaus, particularly the Ministry of Finance and the Ministry of Foreign Affairs. Every one of them needs the favorable patronage of a top-ranking official who can support his career development or assume the necessary expenditure for his climb to the top.

It is not unusual for a man like the Chief of the Secretariat Section to carry a dozen pictures of young women with excellent social backgrounds in his briefcase, for one of his unofficial duties is to arrange meetings between these young women and the elite bachelors. In his briefcase are photos of the daughters of ministers, company presidents, bankers, leaders of political parties, and so on. The bureaucratic go-between makes tenacious approaches to the young elites, because the girls themselves, as well as their parents, long for a match with a man who has a bright future.

In the choice of a lifetime partner, sociability, health, comfort, and other criteria have to be taken into account. This information is usually obtained through the bureaucratic go-between, who carries out the informal personnel administration of the marriage. When a young woman's qualification satisfies a man's ambition and a man's potential for future development satisfies a woman's expectation, the two wed and become a pair. Again, conjugal love is a secondary matter for them to create.

Members of the promising "career group" customarily devote long hours to their work, sacrificing their family life as part of the bravery of modern samurai. Thus their conjugal intimacy at home is greatly cut down. Paucity of vacation is another factor that takes away from home life, so these elite samurai frequently end up being better suited to their official cars than to their wives.

An increasing number of young people insist on finding their own mates, leading to love matches in the Western manner. They no longer feel obliged to bow to family wishes, against their own preferences. At the same time, their parents, who are old-fashioned and keen on finding suitable sons-in-law or daughters-in-law, as well as some prudent young people who wish to widen their cruising radius in the search for better-halves, rely on go-betweens who have broad social connections and accordingly greater capacity to arrange meetings for marriages. On the whole, therefore, the arranged marriage remains more popular in Japan than the love match.

Nowadays the role of these go-betweens is limited. They simply arrange the meeting of a boy and a girl of marriageable age, without seriously taking into account their compatibility and future development. The two meet as candidates for love. On the arranged date, or *miai,* the couple is usually escorted by their parents. If they agree to go further, they will have more frequent dates to deepen their acquaintance. Their association may or may not lead to the final goal of marriage. Each one of them has to make that decision at the first meeting or during the period of association. Either side has a right to say no, but again the decision is often influenced by the opinions of parents or other family members. This continuing regulation of marriage by the family may explain why there is much less pairing off of couples in Japan than in the West. Even in the case of a love match, the couple has to find a temporary "go-between" who plays a central role in the wedding ceremony to launch the couple. Interestingly, the statistics show higher rates of divorce for love matches, despite the initial love and enthusiasm of the couple, than for arranged marriages. Many Japanese feel that family assistance in identifying a suitable mate is quite helpful and healthy.

Marriage for Ancestors

Another distinctive feature of marriage in Japan is its role in perpetuating the "family line" for the ancestors. In a sense, this is part of the Japanese *ie* (family or clan) consciousness, centering on ancestor worship.

A few years ago the following open letter from one young woman appeared in the press:

"There are two daughters in our family and no sons. Our father died when my older sister was eight and I was five. Since that time my poor sister has had to bear the burden of being 'the daughter of one of the oldest families of Edo.' She is now twenty-six and in the teaching profession. She is socially and economically independent. My mother's dearest wish is that she will marry someone as soon as possible so we can adopt him into the family to carry on the family line. The right person has not been found yet. When I think of all the trouble my mother has gone through in raising two children by herself, I cannot make light of her concern for 'the family line.' Still, I want my sister to have a happy marriage, with a husband of her own choice. What is troublesome is the gravity of our ancestors."

This is not a rare case—adoption of a son into a family by marriage. The significance here is that the basis of the Japanese conception of marriage is that a couple serves to carry on the family line. The burden falls mostly on women, who are expected to procreate. In modern Japanese society, blessed with the riches of an advanced material civilization, the number of people who are still seriously concerned with "family lineage" is steadily decreasing. Nevertheless, the family background and educational history of prospective partners are still scrutinized with care and remain a factor in the marital decision. Although love may play a part in it, marriage is, above all, an institution designed to preserve a family's good name.

The mainstay of marriage is love for procreation. At the same time, marriage is for sexual gratification. A newly married couple, whether joining the traditional extended Japanese family or starting one of their own, have a double sex life: procreation and pleasure. This double sexual standard, which leaves men free from the burden of pregnancy and women restricted, is, of course, common throughout the world. As the proverb goes, "Women adventure with men, and men with the world." How is it in Japan? Let us look into the features of married life in the advanced industrial society.

Conjugal Relations

If you are not attractive yourself, it is advantageous for you to go out with someone who is. When a man is seen escorting a good-looking woman, he receives favorable overall ratings from society. Similarly, a man gives a better impression to other people when he has a faithful and helpful wife. Presumably, observers reason that he must have some good qualities to have attracted such a fine woman. The same is true of a woman who has a good husband.

Japanese men and women are very conscious of these effects. However, in the presence of other people, they would never praise their husbands or wives. It is their social etiquette, endorsed by the spirits of Confucianism and *bushidō* (code of the samurai).

In Japanese society, the individual must always adjust his desires to his social environment. People abide by traditional rules that seem, to the Westerner, extremely confining to their emotional life. Strict control of emotion in public is the social duty of every citizen, and husbands and wives as a result are quite shy in their one-to-one relations in public. They tend not to show overt signs of affection in the presence of others. This is, for the most part, a superficial characteristic inherited from an earlier system. We should not fail to notice that there is a strong bond of love between a Japanese husband and wife in spite of their official reserved attitudes.

Controlled Emotion

I was in the departure lobby at the Tokyo Haneda Airport when I suddenly became aware of a woman on the other side of the glass wall. She was sending her farewell to the man standing beside me. They must have been husband and wife, but they were unable to communicate because of the wall and the distance between them. The woman, clad in a kimono, lifted her arm and waved it slightly, her eyes tightly fixed on the man she loved. The man, too, waved his hand slightly in response to her. But their deep love seemed to have penetrated the glass wall and pierced their hearts. The typical shy expressions of love that the couple displayed there concealed the deep affection inside. I was very impressed at the sight. Shyness is an important aspect of human nature and has artistic value, in the sense that there is something hidden behind it.

No matter how good a person's married life is, if he displays his passion blatantly all the time, his flame of passion will probably soon extinguish. A husband and wife would do better to preserve their affection under shyness. I believe this is the art and the secret of success in married life.

> Saying "something to find," my man took me
> To the storeroom away from the gathering.
> He, a soldier tomorrow, embraced me strong,
> At the night of the farewell party.

This is *waka* (a traditional Japanese poem of 31 syllables), taken from the *Showa Manyo-shu* anthology. It was composed by a woman about her husband, who was drafted into World War II. He drew his wife out of the gathering into a dark storeroom and gave her his passionate farewell kiss on departure night. Such controlled emotion is the fundamental quality of conjugal relationships in Japan. The more a couple controls their emotional expression, the more their passion blazes up and ends in gratification when expressed. As a general rule, conjugal attraction is in proportion to the degree of spontaneity between the sexes.

I once lived in Vienna, Austria, next door to a middle-aged couple who seemed very happy. In the morning, before the husband left for work, they hugged each other tightly and exchanged passionate kisses, as if they could not bear their temporary separation. They did it every morning at their doorstep, no matter who was around. "I love you, dear" and "I love you, darling" were the words they exchanged every morning. They probably did the same in the evening when the husband came back home. An ordinary Japanese husband would be worn out if he tried to do the same, even for a week. I often wondered why this couple felt it necessary to express their love so openly every morning and evening. After having lived together for years, any husband and wife should be aware of each other's love and depth of feeling without having to be told in words. A couple should be able to read each other's mind if they are truly married. I thought the Austrian couple's open expression of love was a traditional conjugal greeting. I took it as a cultural habit.

One day, I came across my neighbor in a park and had a chance to talk with him.

"I envy you. You are so together with your wife," I said.

"Oh, no, not really. . . ." My neighbor stuttered and then confessed, "I have to reassure my wife every day by saying 'I love you.' It is the contract between us. I also have to phone her once in a while from my office. Otherwise she grumbles when I come home, and things get extremely hard for me."

He continued, "In fact, I want to divorce her. I have consulted a lawyer, but there seems to be no way out."

I was so astonished by his words that I could not find anything to say. I felt like I had been hit hard on the head. This seemed a perfect example of the husband-and-wife relationship in a contract society. As long as the relationship stays healthy, the contract is the solid source of all happiness, but once the relationship goes sour, the contract can be the source of all troubles. In Japan, there is no particular contract between husband and wife. The social tradition is the rule. They act on the tradition and act as freely as the tradition permits. It is almost impossible for any Japanese man to kiss a woman whom he no longer loves and even wants to divorce.

There seem to be only two seasons, summer and winter, in the contract society, but all four seasons—spring, summer, autumn, and winter—exist in the emotionally charged Japanese society, where self-expression is so delicate and controlled.

Not Sexy but Amorous

Japanese women are not sexy in the manner of women in the West, because the tradition of wearing kimono and obi (wide belt) and sitting upright on the mat floor has shaped their physical proportions differently. However, they have retained a charm by being amorous. Being sexy and being amorous are both sexual appeals, but the two differ greatly. Being sexy is a direct expression of the flesh and body, and this kind of charm usually declines with age. Amorousness, on the other hand, goes beyond the physical. It is a sexual appeal that includes tender-hearted charm. A woman therefore can be amorous at any age, as long as she keeps up her appearance and mingles her physical attractiveness with a charming personality. Amorousness can develop into eroticism—not in the sense of indecency but in the sense of eros, or pleasure-directed self-expression (from Eros, the Greek God of Love).

During World War II, in a South Sea island occupied by the Japanese forces, the army ordered the native women, who were wearing nothing but a piece of cloth around their waists, to dress more decorously in order to upgrade the public morality. To great surprise, the men began to complain that the women, wearing dresses and showing their legs now and then when the hems turned up gracefully as they walked, were too stimulating to them. The nude women were more natural on the island and therefore less tempting for the men. This suggests that amorousness—the hint of physicality—is a more effective and lasting sexual appeal than nudity.

Iki

In the case of Japanese women, lovely bare feet clad in red-thonged black-lacquered clogs peeking out from a kimono are more appealing and charming than the bare shoulders of those wearing open summer dresses. This indefinable quality of being amorous is called *iki* and is considered a refined degree of charm in Japan. The first requirement for *iki*, according to *Anatomy of Iki* by Shuzo Kuki, is coquetry, and the second requirement is "spirit, or temperament." If the meaning of *iki* were simply "sensuality" or "amorous flirtation," many Western words would suffice to describe it. But the fact that there is no Western equivalent suggests that *iki*, as Shuzo Kuki states, is a psychological phenomenon alien to Western culture. *Iki* is a combination of amorous flirtation and controlled self-expression, manifested outward as a single activity. It is the irrepressible eros of the self which runs through the quality of sexual appeal.

The figure of a Japanese woman walking with swaying steps in her casual kimono after her bath is *iki*. Likewise, the figure of a Western woman in her evening dress with her upper breasts exposed is erotic and amorous. Such exposure of a woman's physical self represents a sort of *iki*, a sensual liberality. Yet something is missing to be true *iki*,

Mr. Kuki cites "resignation" as the third requirement for *iki*, but I would not use this term. Rather, I would call it refinement—a chic and tasteful spirit emanating from an erotic attitude. Examples are the Japanese woman cited above, fresh from her bath, and the geisha entertaining at a banquet. They offer fine testimony to this quality. The geisha's collar is tilted just a bit to the back—a glimpse of her neck is the only hint of flesh under the kimono. This is quite different from the open neckline or bare back of the modern Western woman in her evening dress. The geisha's modest exposure of eros represents her controlled self inside. Though the eros is expressed, it is an extremely refined and controlled erotic attitude.

The critical point is that the geisha reveals her eros only to the extent that her self-control and natural moderation command her—"I will show just this much of my flesh, and nothing more!" The difference between the frank sexuality of a modern woman and the faint suggestion of sensuality of a classic woman is the difference between self-assertion and self-control. A wink is a bit too strong to be *iki;* a sidelong glance could be. Refined amorousness can be depicted only in such a self-controlled manner. Mr. Kuki's "resignation" perhaps refers to this self-control, which recognizes the futility of the open eros.

Iki, then, is a unique combination of amorousness, spirit, and self-control. Obviously, this is a very difficult set of qualities to cultivate and sustain. Self-control, the third component of *iki,* is especially difficult for the maturing woman to learn. Only those who dedicate themselves entirely to refinement can embody *iki* successfully.

Here it might be interesting to discuss another Japanese word, *nama-iki* (sauciness or insolence; literally, "raw iki"). *Nama-iki* is the vain attempt to exhibit *iki* by someone who just does not have it. Such a person is confident of her (or his) own appeal but lacks recognition of that quality by society. Lack of social recognition is what turns would-be *iki* into *nama-iki.* It is *iki* lacking the all-important quality of self-control. *Nama-iki* is much closer to *iki's* antonym, *yabo* (rusticity, uncouthness), than it is to *iki* itself. In Japan there is a saying, "The rustic gets polished into a sophisticate." In other words, the person who is *nama-iki* gains refinement by coming in contact with society, eventually gaining its recognition and approval and thereby becoming *iki.*

There is another Japanese saying, "If you speak up, you're considered *nama-iki* (insolent); if you keep silent, you're considered ignorant." How accurately this describes the dilemma of the modern Japanese businessman in the hierarchical society. Mere silence no longer suffices as a response to the remarks of one's superior. The businessman is expected to be dynamic as well as reserved, and to say what needs to be said, but in the proper way.

Refining the self to be *iki* is the key to a successful married life. Expressing anything timely in the proper amount is true *iki*, and it requires the unmitigated efforts of a married couple to attain.

Ki and Freedom

The English word "spirit" and the French word "esprit" are usually translated into Japanese as *seishin,* but in my opinion the word *ki* is a better translation. According to the *kojien* (a Japanese dictionary), *ki* means (1) the mental activity that is the primal force of life; (2) the activity of the mind in general. Synonyms for *ki* include reason, emotion, will, intention, conscience, spirit, disposition, and nature.

Many Japanese expressions are built around the word *ki: ki ga susuma nai* (I don't feel like doing anything); *ki ga chiru* (to be distracted); *ki ga meiru* (to feel depressed); *ki ga ki de nai* (to feel uneasy); *ki wa kokoro* (to have goodwill); *ki o torinaosu* (to brace oneself); *ki ga tooku naru* (to feel faint); *ki ga tsuku* (to notice); *ki ga kiku* (to be considerate); *ki ga hikeru* (to feel inferior); and *ki ga nukeru* (to be dispirited).

Beer that has lost its *ki* (*ki no nuketa bīru*) is beer without punch, and it is a dull drink. A spiritless answer (*ki no nai henji*) is a reply without any feeling, and like beer without the carbonation it is dull. Spiritless writing (*kak-ki no nai bunsho*) is a literary style without force or energy. *Ki* in all these phrases represents the spirit at the center of something, especially at the core of human feeling.

My next example may take your breath away, but because it is an apt metaphor for the freedom the human spirit craves, I see no reason to hesitate. There is an expression in Japanese that you won't find in the dictionary: *ki ga iku* (literally, "the spirit goes").

This expression has an English equivalent in which the direction is typically reversed: the slang expression "to come." In Japanese, the vulgarism *ki ga iku* is used to indicate sexual climax, a peak state for the entire body. However, the expression is generally limited to cases of mutual orgasm and is not used to refer to ejaculation by masturbation. It expresses great freedom—not freedom in isolation, but freedom in the embrace of a partner. When both parties reach a climax at the same time, the Japanese say, *ki ga au* (spirits meet, or match). This is the most desired state, the state of total release that all human beings desire. Of course, this freedom of release is not available in sexual assault, or in sexual activity without love.

The expression *ki ga au* is not limited to descriptions of sexual climax. It can be used to refer to the "meeting of minds" that occurs whenever two partners work together with complete mutual satisfaction. In practice, the expression is used even more casually, to mean "we see eye to eye," "we understand each other," or "we can work together." In any case, the essential meaning of the phrase is two free minds meeting, communing, and finding mutual satisfaction with the implication that true human freedom never exists in isolation. True freedom is achieved by doing what you want while harmonizing with others and staying in tune with your surroundings.

Of course, this freedom is not easy to attain. A look at the word *kimama* makes this clear. *Kimama* means "just as your spirit wants"; it is self-indulgence, or the pursuit of self-satisfaction. Retiring to a mountain hut and living exactly as you please might seem like a paradise, but unless you can also eliminate all worldly desires, you won't achieve true freedom. If the slightest wish or desire intrudes on you, you will be driven to dissatisfaction by the principle of *kimama* and will soon be unable to enjoy anything.

At any rate, very few people these days try to find their freedom by eliminating desires. Instead, they seek their freedom within society by trying to satisfy all their desires in a patently self-indulgent manner. Self-indulgence *(kimama)* becomes selfishness very easily and never gets satisfied.

The Magic of Language

According to Pavlov's "conditioned response," dogs can be taught to salivate at the sound of a bell. We human beings are more complex than dogs and have been conditioned to react to many things, but our strongest reactions are probably to words. We react to words more powerfully than to anything else.

The Japanese language contains many emotionally charged words. Since they are emotionally subtle, they often sound delicate and ambiguous. And people's reactions vary according to their interpretations of the words.

In a homogeneous society like Japan, where people are not very different from each other in their ways of thinking, communications do not have to be very explicit or precise. In the case of husbands and wives especially, communication need not always be fully worded. Husband and wife are so in tune with each other that things often go smoothly between them without many words. At the same time, in a society where delicacy and sensitivity to feelings are such important parts of human relationships, the use of words is very crucial and difficult. The emotionally charged Japanese language embodies a lot of magic power, and people need to be aware of this magic power in their choice of words. The language has, as clearly revealed in the literature, a rich variety of words denoting subtle esthetic and emotional states.

Words of Affection

Emotion is an important element of any culture, and people represent their emotions in words. In Japanese, different words are used by men and by women, whereas in Western societies the same words can be used by both sexes. The use of Japanese words is quite complicated, as stated in the previous chapter.

Not only do the words used by men and women differ, but a number of words take different forms for different situations and relationships between the speaker and the listener or the person referred to. For example, there are many words for "you"—*omae, kimi, anata, kisama, anata-sama,* and so on. And certain words are used only between a husband and wife to express their delicate conjugal relationships.

Omae (you) is a popular form of address by a husband to his wife. However, there is some controversy over this word. Those who favor using *omae* reason that it conveys feelings of "dignity," "warmth," and "intimacy." Those who dislike *omae,* most of whom are among the younger generation, argue that it carries connotations of "domination" and "superiority"—a husband being above a wife—and "boastfulness." Both arguments do not make much difference to the many husbands who have been using *omae* as a convention for years. Another word meaning "you" now often used by young husbands is *kimi,* which has a friendlier sound but lacks dignity.

In fact, the word *omae* is used by a man in two cases: when calling another male rather rudely on an equivalent level and when calling his wife. Thus *omae,* when the "you" is female, can be used only by a husband addressing his own wife. In other words, there is only one man in the world who can call a woman *omae;* that is her husband. Although *omae* does convey a nuance of domination or rudeness, it is the privilege of a husband to use this word. In a sense, *omae* symbolizes the happy monopoly of the marital relationship.

Anata (you) is the word most commonly used by a woman to address her husband. However, *anata* is not restricted to a marriage partner: it can be used to address any person of either sex, of any age. And anybody, not only the wife, can call the husband *anata*. It may seem unfair for the wife not to have a monopoly over *anata*, while the husband has a special privilege over *omae*. However, *anata* used by a dearest wife to call her husband sounds emotionally different from *anata* used by people in other situations. The special tone of affection put into *anata* by the wife drives the heart of the husband. Her willingness to be his wife and her love toward him are contained in the word, and her lovely tone can never be copied by others. Like *omae, anata* expresses the conjugal intimacy between husband and wife.

Another controversial Japanese word is *shujin*, which originally meant "master." This term is traditionally used by a wife to introduce her husband in conversations. However, some women protest its use, arguing that a husband is not a master of his wife. Others reason that *shujin* is just an idiom for the head of a family, just as *kanai* (inside of house), when used by a husband, refers to a wife who stays home. Being fussy about words that have lost their original meaning seems rather pointless.

Several other words can be used in place of *shujin—otō-san* (father), *papa, danna, teishu*—none of which, however, sound as dignified. Probably the best way for a woman to refer to her husband is by *uchi-no hito* (my dear man). And a man usually presents his wife by *uchi-no yatsu* (my dear wife), though *yatsu* again carries a sense of intimate rudeness. These expressions are conventional in a Japanese family and do not convey any disrespect.

Voiceless Affection

Everyone has experienced an uncontrollable desire to talk to someone else. That desire arises from the innermost self.

Wives who stay at home alone while their husbands and children are out during the day become victims of such a desire at least once or twice a day and end up in a hen party or long chatting sessions over the phone. This desire to communicate is similar to the desire to escape from solitude.

Japanese husbands feel such a desire in the evening when they are about to go home after a busy day's work. This is because during the day at the office, they take care not to slip any extra words into their official communications. When they are released in the evening, they become extremely thirsty for "free, open-minded communication." Furthermore, the superficial "public front" communication in the office is not enough for them to obtain information on "what's going on behind the scenes"—information they need in order to compete with their colleagues on the organizational ladder. As a result, they hurry, by twos and threes, to taverns and pubs for "businessmen's drinks" on the way home. There, in a totally different atmosphere, they enjoy informal communication. They murmur and gossip, trying to snatch useful information from colleagues while exchanging jokes with the tavern hostesses. The husbands, therefore, usually fulfill their desire to communicate by talking freely over drinks before they get home.

A wife often meets the wooden face of her husband at the door when he comes home late at night. He just gives her a glance and says, "Ah-h-h, dear me!" Many times, this is the only communication between them. The husband really disappoints his wife, who might even have arranged some flowers to welcome him home. If this attitude becomes habitual on his part, his wife and children will become frustrated in their desire to communicate with him. However, the samurai husband is not supposed to chat in a merry voice with his wife.

One Japanese wife told me this story:

"I had everything I want. The only problem was that my husband kept his words to a minimum every day, saying no more than was absolutely necessary. There was very limited communication between us. I really could not know what was on his mind and I was always unsure of his love toward me. [A Japanese husband usually does not express his love for his wife in words.] One day, I fell ill and was admitted to a hospital for a while. Not only did my husband come to visit me every day but he was extremely kind and took great care of me. This was more than enough to assure me of his love. I am now really happy, though his verbal communication is still limited."

This woman is one of the many Japanese wives who are frustrated by the voiceless communication of their husbands. Everyone needs to communicate his or her true self to someone. This is one reason people get married. Japanese husbands need to take off their samurai masks more often and show themselves to their wives, though by Confucian tradition they are supposed to express their love in deeds, beyond others' awareness. Of course, when husband and wife are together at home, they are able to read each other's minds without many words and need not give constant reassurances of their love. Even so, some verbal communication between husband and wife in this complex society is important if they are to fully exchange minds and hearts.

An open letter from one Japanese wife in a women's magazine reveals her mind:

"I wish to have an intelligent conversation once in a while with my husband; the chance ripens after the children have gone to bed. However, my husband does not respond to my attempt. I perhaps made a mistake in choosing my man." In the tradition of the feudalistic age, many Japanese men are still samurai with their wives.

Unilateral Affection in Deeds

A few years ago, one manufacturer of shoeshine cream carried out a questionnaire survey of 20,000 wives (ranging in age from the teens to the fifties). The question was "What do you do for your husband every morning?" The following replies were returned:

1. Polish his shoes (4,770 cases).
   No doubt, the fact that the surveyor was a shoe cream manufacturer influenced some of these replies, so we should discount the given number to some extent.
2. Prepare breakfast for him (3,773 cases).
   All over the world, this is quite an ordinary task for housewives in the morning, is it not?
3. Help him dress for the day (2,030 cases).
   This is not unusual for an ordinary Japanese wife.
4. Prepare his lunch (1,341 cases).
   Japanese husbands do not come home for lunch like Europeans, because of the long commuting distances and short lunch hours. And even though there are company dining halls and many restaurants in town, a few of them still take their lunches, prepared by their wives, to work.
5. Check his belongings and supplement any insufficiency (1,011 cases).
   Japanese wives consider it a duty to assist their husbands in the morning in getting ready for work. Most wives see that their husbands are fully equipped for the day's battle.
6. See him off at the front door (855 cases).
   This was a formality in the Tokugawa samurai society and is a common practice among Japanese wives today.
7. Wake him up gently (521 cases).
   Many husbands are sleepy heads because of their daily hard work and their personal meetings in the evening.
8. Prepare coffee or tea for him (378 cases).
   This is not at all unusual. I wonder why there were only 378 cases.
9. Arrange a pair of shoes to match his suit (378 cases).
   This takes some artistic sense.
10. Iron his shirt and trousers (377 cases).
    His appearance is her appearance in Japan. A fastidious wife is greatly appreciated by the society.
11. Bring newspapers in from the mailbox (321 cases).
    The wife wants her husband to read all the important information before he engages in the battle of the day.
12. Set up his motorbike or start the engine of his car (321 cases).

Many, if not most, Japanese wives are eager to be good assistants to their husbands. A wife starts her husband's spiritual engine for the day.

13. Select his tie for the day and knot it up at his neck (238 cases).

    The husband can enjoy this service every morning but must remember that his wife holds an advantage here in that she can strangle him with his tie.

14. Arrange washroom gadgets and toiletries for him (187 cases).

    A wife saves a great deal of her husband's time. The queen keeps the king on schedule in the morning.

15. Prepare hot bean paste soup for him (180 cases).

    Bean paste soup made from soy beans is a typical Japanese breakfast.

16. Say *itteras-shai* (literally, "please go off"; meaning "see you again at home") with a smile (157 cases).

    Her smile must be a charming one, but the samurai's face must remain dignified. In the Tokugawa period, Confucianism taught the Japanese samurai not to express four emotions—*ki* (joy), *do* (anger), *ai* (sorrow), and *raku* (comfort)—on his face. Even today the tradition compels a man to remain emotionally reticent.

17. Prepare vegetable and fruit juice for him (152 cases).

    A married man is never ill fed or underfed in Japan. He is a very important earning machine for the family.

18. Give him clean underwear (137 cases).

    It would be the wife's shame in Japan if her husband's dirty underwear happened to be exposed to the eyes of others.

19. Lay out his hair dryer for him (113 cases).

    Here again, the queen keeps the king on schedule by saving him time.

20. Remind him of the time by shouting loudly to him while he is in the toilet (76 cases).

    This resembles the cheerful wife shown in the American comicstrip "Blondie."

21. Spray perfume over him (2 cases).

    Many Japanese wives earnestly intend to be the architects of their husbands' appearance.

22. Bother to put his socks on his legs and to hurry him up (1 case).

    To be punctual, a man needs a wife in Japan.
23. Spray eau de cologne in his armpit (1 case).

    Such a tender-hearted service is not an amazing gesture in any part of the world, but if it is done every morning, that is something.
24. Hold his hands gracefully and ask what time he will come back home (1 case).

    This is the most effective way of enchanting a samurai's heart, because the wife's affectionate deed strengthens the magic of her words, and her words vitalize her deed.

Although this survey is a few years old and the figures from it are not entirely accurate, they do give us a good picture of how helpful Japanese wives are and how fortunate their husbands are. In the isolated islands, the Tokugawa feudal system placed women under men and created better wives and worse husbands in the process. The imbalance remains because no other alternative has ever taken root. The findings from this survey might well lead us to conclude that Japan's tremendous development was achieved not only by the samurai workers but also by their wives. Half the credit surely goes to the housewives. Their quality control of husbands has been excellent.

The Divided Frame of Life

In *bushidō* (the code of the samurai), the loyal devotion of a samurai to his lord was essential. The alpha and omega of a samurai's life was service—nothing but self-sacrificing service to his lord. To a samurai, the pledge of loyalty was everything. A samurai gave himself up in toto to his lord. Therefore he did not even consider enjoying his home life and the conjugal love of his wife. A samurai's wife was also inculcated to support the loyal devotion of her husband to his lord. Accordingly, the life of a couple was divided: the husband's place was with the lord and the wife's place was in the home. Because deep conjugal relationships tended to weaken the samurai's spirit and cause him to neglect his duty, *bushidō* proscribed such intimate relationships. Humanistic love was denied in order to keep the samurai ready to renounce his life at any time for the sake of his lord.

Japan has been changing fast, but a remnant of the samurai spirit exists steadfastly in the hearts of men. Japanese men are fearful of being looked down upon or being called a sissy by others for showing their conjugal intimacy in public. So are women, when they are out with their men. The open expression of conjugal love is not part of Japanese tradition.

I can remember well that before the war a woman was likely to follow deferentially a step behind her husband on the street, carrying their baby or bundles, while he walked ahead in lordly fashion. Since the war, great changes have taken place and women have won greater equality with men. The new way of thinking holds that there should be a stronger and more open bond of love between a husband and a wife. They now walk side by side, and their baby or bundles are often in his arms, not in hers. An increasing number of husbands now help out their wives with the evening dishes. However, this is a phenomenon among young couples and is only a superficial indication of change. Most of the traditional ways remain. If a middle-aged man like me were to go swimming with his wife unaccompanied by their children, it would cause a sensation all over the community. My wife and I did so once, and the next day my wife was asked by other housewives in the neighborhood: "Is it true that you went swimming with your husband?" They sounded as if we had done something wrong. The reader can imagine how much bigger a splash my wife would have made in Japanese society if she had gone swimming with another man. In Western society, a woman could probably boldly say "It's none of your business," even in such a clear case of social immorality. In the traditional Japanese society, the wife would stand at bay, and might even have to commit suicide.

In Japan, it is not yet a social custom for a man to take his wife to parties. The parties are usually attended by men only, and sometimes office girls as well. Even on occasions when outside guests are cordially invited, wives are rarely, if ever, asked to attend with their husbands. The husbands go out, the wives stay at home—this is the typical scenario in Japan. The other day an American woman married to a Japanese man lamented the situation as follows in the press:

"Upon coming to Japan a couple of years ago, I was disappointed to find that the 'comfortable little group' attitude prevails in this country, not just to foreigners but to anyone outside the group. And the most obvious 'outsiders' in Japan are the women. For the most part, men in Japan do not associate with women. The business world is almost exclusively male, and social contacts seem limited to after-hours drinking with associates and Sunday golf or some such activity with old school friends or club acquaintances."

When Japanese executives go abroad on business, they often come back deeply impressed by the capable wives in Western society who, in the company of their husbands at a social affair, manage the party or otherwise do their part efficiently. The executives say, "Why don't we have such 'Missuses' in Japan?" It is not a question of "we have" or "we don't have." Japanese wives are simply not given the chance to become socially capable. And that is the fault of their husbands. The worlds of Japanese husband and wife have been sharply divided for many centuries. Therefore, there have been excellent housewives in Japan but very few efficient "Missuses" who are socially capable.

Self-Sacrifice Under Industrial Feudalism

Employees of a Japanese company are just like the samurai of the Tokugawa period. They are enclosed for a lifetime in the castle (the enterprise). Their single-hearted loyalty to the lord (top management) is essential. The high spirits and self-sacrifice of the samurai were extremely favorable to Japan's making a start as a modern state in the Meiji era and then carrying out a reconstruction and further economic development in the postwar period. Quite a few examples in earlier chapters have demonstrated this.

Here is a statement that a middle-aged housewife made in a magazine several years ago:

"My husband is now over forty years old but still works incredibly hard. He leaves home at 6:30 every morning and hardly ever comes home before midnight. Over the last two weeks, he came home three days at 1:00 A.M., five days at 2:00 A.M., and two days at 4:00 A.M. Over the weekends, as a result, he just sleeps, sleeps, and sleeps. All he says to me every day is, 'I must work, I must work. Oh, I am too busy!' Now I'm not so ignorant as to believe all these words. He works very hard every day for his company, which in turn provides him with enjoyable drinks after work. He never entertains his two children and me; nor does he buy clothing to please us. We are just fed and have enough to live on. The rest of his income is spent on the social activities of the evening. The days have passed like this for fifteen years. I have been suffering much, but seem to have gotten used to it. I am now able to look at it objectively from a different angle, and complain less about my family life to my sisters and friends. I no longer try to correct my husband's life or blame the company for its working standards. I have resigned myself to my fate and accepted it as inevitable. I just hope that my children will not grow up to be like their father."

This is an extreme case and a rare one. This man is one of

the world's great "workaholics." But there are many lesser work-aholics who sacrifice their home lives for their work. Hard work is the pride of the samurai worker. Employment is not only his lifeblood but a centrally significant "good" for him. Japanese men place primary importance on their castle (place of employment), and their homes accordingly become mere lodging places for them to sleep in and commute from. The wife of the vice president of a big trading company, a man victimized in an aircraft scandal, once described her husband this way in a magazine: "He lodged in my house for twenty years." If this was true of the vice president, no doubt those who worked under him also lodged in their houses just for sleep and devoted themselves unconditionally to the company.

The organizational style of Japanese enterprises today is very similar to the Tokugawa system of *han* (feudal clan). The employer-employee relationship is rooted in that between the ruler and the ruled of the clan. The relationship is based on *on* (social debt handed down by a favor), not on a contract.

The Western employer-employee contract can be fulfilled by the equalizing of work and wages, but *on* between ruler and ruled is usually limitless and never can be paid off. The suicide note left by an ex-councilor who was involved in the bribery scandal of KDD (International Telecommunications Incorpo-rated) manifests such a feudalistic relationship. It read, in part:

"I was just an ordinary man of no special ability. I owe the former president and the former general secretary a great deal. By their favor, at my retirement at age fifty-eight, I was given a special post as the so-called councilor in the president's office. After that time, I was filled with a zeal to repay their favor, and I tried my best to follow their directions. In this case, too, I was only trying to make up for the delinquencies of the two. . . ."

In the contract-based society of the West, when an employee is asked to commit an unlawful act, he can refuse by saying, "That is not part of my job description." But this is not possible in

Japanese society. In a feudalistic system, there is no job description. All orders given by a senior are duties. An employee has to go beyond his regular commitment if he is to succeed. Anyone who fails to take on extra work as required temporarily, and instead punches a time clock at nine in the morning and again at five, becomes an outcast.

Two Homes

The Japanese worker has two "homes." One is the residence he shares with his wife and the other is his workplace, which he considers his central life station. When a worker speaks of his company, he always refers to it as *uchi-no-kaisha* (literally, "my company"; practically, "my dear company," for *uchi-no* implies an intimacy of kinship). The company is like a home for most of the men, in much the same way as the samurai regarded the lord's castle as their central life station. In fact, modern Japanese workers usually spend more time in their workplace than in their homes.

A typical Japanese company has numerous characters: a community mayor, an old-timer, a big shot, friends, brothers-in-work, sisters-in-work, seniors, juniors, and so on. In other words, the company is a village-type community. There are also festive activities, protocols, and customs. No definite line separates official and personal affairs. Such a system, of course, may become a source of friction among workers, but at the same time it provides them with plenty of opportunities to assuage the wounds and sorrows of the working class. The worker can borrow his pay in advance, deposit his savings in a company fund at a better interest rate than a bank provides, drink at company expense, receive loans from the company for buying a house, and complain to his colleagues about what he cannot disclose to his wife. Naturally, such workers stay with the same employer much longer than workers do in the West. Japanese employees repeatedly say, "*Uchi-no-kaisha, uchi-no-kaisha.*" The company is no less than the control tower of their lives. It is like a spiritual harbor for floating souls. The loyalty of Japanese workers resides in this strong sense of belongingness, of being part of an organization in which all members' destinies are tightly interlocked.

This is why Japanese husbands spend most of their time away from their families. In nine cases out of ten, they are occupied by affairs of the company. The wives, on the other hand, stay at home and have no idea of their husbands'- jobs. They do not know the men's world. Of course, the wife of a shop owner may have a chance to see her husband at work, but most husbands work at offices, stores, or plants, and seldom talk about their struggles in the battlefield when they return home. Since this has been true for many years, Japanese wives are not necessarily dissatisfied and never try to lure their husbands away from the lord and castle.

Instead, the wives focus their energies on the family. They take up bravely the entire burden of providing nurturance and education for their children, all the way from infancy to adulthood. Such mothers are called "education mamas" in Japan, and they are the chief promoters of the notorious "examination hell" that Japanese students go through. Their great task is to ensure that their offspring get into the right kindergarten, then into the right primary school, then into the right junior high school, then into the right senior high school, and then into the right university. Their purpose in sending their children to the right schools is, needless to say, to install them in stable jobs with big companies and get them on the promotional escalator. The future of the children is calculated beforehand by their mothers, who devote all their energies to the task. Lacking the confident helping hand of their husbands, these women find it very difficult to cut the umbilical cord.

Role of Partners

In ancient times, women were engaged solely in housework and rearing infants, and men in the struggle with neighboring tribes and wild animals and in hunting game for the family. Men's duty was always very risky and involved desperate life-or-death confrontations. As long as men were engaged in such dangerous work, in which women could not participate, there was no room for a women's liberation movement to develop. The roles of men and women were clearly separated.

With the progress of civilization, men's work has been rationalized and simplified, and men are no longer required to face life-threatening danger. In contrast, women must still undergo the burdens and pains of pregnancy and childbirth, though they have been greatly relieved of housework as a result of modern science.

Today, men play their role outside the home as they did in ancient times, but it is no longer a matter of life or death. They can even afford to read papers or magazines on the commuter train to work and can enjoy a drink on the way home. Women's position too has changed. They now have an opportunity to do many of the same things as men. In fact, many women are doing as well as or sometimes even better than their male counterparts in Japanese society. It is natural that the women's upheaval will continue.

Nevertheless, in a traditional society like Japan, there is still a distinct boundary between the roles of husband and wife. They may be trapped by their own notions of "manliness" or "womanliness," but a more fundamental point seems to be that Japanese women are proud of their dominant family role in keeping the household together while the men go out and earn a livelihood outside. Judging from the fact that Japanese wives usually have absolute control over the family budget and the education of children, along with a responsibility to hold the family together, they are definitely the "stronger sex" in the family. Despite their subservient manner, the position of Japanese wives is something more than it has often seemed to be. In addition, despite the heavy overlay of male supremacy resulting from feudalistic and Confucian concepts, Japanese husbands very often demonstrate weaknesses of personality. They wish to be the wives' grown-up children and are lost without their tender care. A Japanese man, once experienced as a husband, cannot survive without a wife, whereas women have proved that they can lead a single life after divorce or the death of a spouse. Japanese wives have more will power and psychological strength than their husbands, and it may even be concluded that these wives—the "stronger sex"— are the mainstay of Japanese society.

Expectations of a Wife

One night I telephoned a friend of mine after I had returned home. It was around nine o'clock, which I thought was not too early and not too late to catch him. His wife came on the phone and said to me:

"My husband? He is always Gozensama [Mr. A.M.]. O ho ho ho ho. . . ." She laughed happily and proudly. Gozensama is the nickname for a husband who comes home after midnight. It means automatically that he is a hard worker and has a sign of success in life. It also means that he is a loyal samurai to his lord. This wife's happy laughter obviously came from her confidence that her husband's deep involvement with his work was putting him well on the road to success.

"In contrast to my husband, you are already home. How hopeless you are. . . ." She did not say this exactly in words, but her triumphant laughter surely implied it.

The American billionaire J. Paul Getty, who passed away some years ago, was married and divorced five times in his life. In his book *How to Be Rich,* he explained why his five marriages ended in failure. Each of his former wives was a wonderful woman who did her utmost to make their marriage a success. But he overworked. He could not remember taking a single day of vacation in 45 years. His work schedule and need to devote most of his time to building and expanding his businesses took a heavy toll on his personal life. When each of his wives found her man thinking of his business interests first and of her only second, she could not feel she was really a wife, or that she really had a husband.

I imagine Getty would not have been divorced if he had had a Japanese wife. In general, a Japanese wife would be pleased to support such a great samurai husband as long as he showed a promising future. She would feel better knowing that her husband was dedicating so much of his time to business achievement. Japanese wives are usually more understanding of their husbands than are wives in the West and put up with a considerable degree of hardship and solitude for the sake of their husbands' career. Perhaps no other women in the world are so anxious for the success of their husbands as are Japanese wives. Why is this so?

Japanese women have been tied to the traditional family system for centuries. Doomed to stay inside the house, they were denied any important social participation. Therefore, a wife needed a surrogate to express her existence and aspirations socially. Her husband has always played this role and been her chief status symbol. Success or failure of the husband has always had grave significance for the wife. If the husband rises in his career, the wife will be credited by the community with an invisible but honorable award entitled "meritorious supporter." This is an uncontestable social identity for a married woman. The more boring and tedious housework is, the more the wife desires her husband to work harder and achieve more.

Mr. A was a good-natured man who graduated from a

first-rate university and then went to work for a well-known trading company. He was rather serious-minded, and his image was more that of an intellectual than of a businessman. Several years after his marriage, he was transferred from a top-level sales job in the field to a desk job in personnel. The transfer indicated that he was no longer a promising samurai executive.

When he was 45, his wife foresaw that he would rise no higher in the company than to the position of section chief. Thereafter, she began to develop strange physical symptoms. Her husband's very approach to her made her sick. She could not help feeling a disgusting chill and could not stop shivering for a while. Merely thinking of her husband's future gave her a fierce headache. To make matters worse, one day in Ginza (a famous shopping street in Tokyo) she attended the alumni meeting of her university classmates. Each one of them spoke about her chief status symbol—her husband: professor, doctor, big businessman, bureau director, and so on. The sexual relationship between Mr. and Mrs. A ceased for good after that. Mrs. A began torturing her husband over the smallest matter. What terrible days the husband had to go through! Even the slightest retort on his part made her hysterical. She would faint and her hands and feet got stiff. Later her illness became worse and she was admitted to the hospital.

This is an extreme and rare case, but it does illustrate the high expectations a Japanese wife has for her husband. It is only a matter of degree. The development and progress of the husband is everything for the wife. An average husband is just like a runner on a jogging machine. He keeps running on the conveyor belt of the machine—runs, runs, and runs—but never reaches the goal: satisfying the expectations of his wife. And her nagging at him never improves the situation. It only drives him to be another Gozensama, who sacrifices his family life and works harder.

Expectations of a Husband

For many young men, sexual attractiveness is a primary criterion in the choice of a partner. The determining factor for them is usually a woman's physical features—a good-looking face, large breasts, and full hips set against a narrow waist. However, when mature men are asked to give qualities they regard as most important in their marriage partners, virtues such as tender-heartedness, sincerity, faithfulness, and warmth are often cited, and the commodity value of physical attractiveness is usually given secondary importance.

In Japan, a man's most important expectation in a woman is domesticity. In forming a lifetime partnership, a Japanese man, who should have a promising future, requires his partner to be entirely domestic to support him in his climb. It is typical for a Japanese boy to make this kind of calculation in preparing for his career and lifetime partnership. This is because it has been proved in Japan's long history that a domestic wife contributes the most to a husband's career and to the success of the pairing in general.

What, then, is "being domestic" in Japanese terms? Why do men want that quality in their lifetime partners? "Being domestic" is a safeguard for men who spend most of the day outside their homes. They want good housekeepers to look after their home and children. If the wife is clumsy in housecleaning, lazy in cooking, and reluctant to wash clothes and dishes, a man's home life will be miserable and his love for his wife will almost certainly diminish day after day—regardless of how sociable, talented, or attractive the wife is. The husband will probably be inclined to envy other husbands who have domestic wives. This phenomenon is not unusual in Japan. Quite a few husbands eat a quick breakfast at a kiosk in a train station, or purchase some ready-made food for the family supper on the way home. Their faces do not look blissful at all. It is very difficult to find a domestic wife in today's affluent society, which has so many devices to replace housework: laundries, instant foods, cleaning agencies, day care centers, and so on.

Under such social conditions, the quality of being domestic not only has greater value but has taken on broader meaning. Rather than merely being a good housekeeper, a wife is now expected to have the psychological qualities needed to hold the family together. She needs to be broad-minded, warm, cheerful, and tolerant of her husband and children. She cannot achieve such virtues simply by staying inside and doing housework. She has to understand all sorts of things around her and her family. She should be sociable and knowledgeable, and also available to her family. At the same time, she should be a dominant ruler of the family.

Mr. B was a white-collar worker and a hardworking man. One day he was transferred to a new post—apparently a demotion—following the merger of his company with a larger one. He was one of the victims of reorganization. When he returned home, he told his wife all about it and lamented what had happened. His wife was surprised and mortified at his demotional transfer but she was clever and suppressed her emotion.

"Oh, dear, that's not so bad! You get paid without working as hard as before. That's even wonderful, isn't it?" She abandoned her expectation of many years and tried to cheer him up and heal his wounded spirit. Despite his wife's effort, he only continued to sigh deeply. For more than ten years, he had devoted himself completely to the company, sacrificing his family life for the sake of his job. The reward he received was a merciless demotion. Throughout that period, his wife had managed all the household duties and the rearing of their children. He owed her very much for his happy home life.

One week and two weeks passed. The children started romping about their father saying, "How nice! Daddy is on vacation." His wife was wise in comforting him every evening when he came home.

"Company life is not the only source of worth for you. Men become aware of their stupidity in working so hard only after they are completely worn out. You are fortunate because you have been thrown out of the fray early." At least at home he could feel comforted.

It may be said that the most domestic wife is one like Mrs. B who is able to relieve the mind of a husband who has been defeated by the organization. Mrs. B tried hard to endow her husband with a new pride and to revitalize his defeated spirit. This ability to offer psychological support is the quality every man looks for in a wife. Perhaps he wishes subconsciously to be mothered by her, and he turns to her for tender care. This is the dependence syndrome. Naturally, the expectation of a husband contradicts the chronic "success" expectation of a wife, described previously in the story of Mrs. A. A wise wife, however, is able to abandon her expectation, like Mrs. B, whenever circumstances require. She becomes truly domestic by giving up her expectation. Thus the contradiction between the expectation of a husband and that of a wife is usually overcome by the domestic wife in Japan.

Social Role of a Housewife

From the above description, the reader can easily imagine that the diligence of Japanese workers is fully supported by their wives and that Japan's industrial strength is maintained by the semimystical power of these housewives. Japan owes them very much indeed. They never complain about tedious work. They seldom become sulky. They are totally self-sacrificing. It is because of them that the husbands can devote themselves wholeheartedly to their work. Although they are very domestic, they have contributed greatly to the success of Japanese industrial society. In this sense, they are important social contributors.

Recently, however, quite a few women have begun to struggle against the wall that confines them to the house. In Japan, these women are referred to as "women who have flown the coop." They want to be independent, and masters of themselves. Very often they are described as career girls or career women. These women are determined to meet the world on its own terms, and to win independence on their own merits. They cannot have true independence without economic independence—this is their belief.

In the context of Japanese society, this is a wonderful ambition. But should a woman's pride or worth be measured solely by economic independence? Also, is it not a profound error to regard every aspect of married life as subservience to the male? The meaning of "subservience" is quite different for each couple. A wise woman can build a married life that is not subservient to her husband. A wife is considered economically dependent for the simple reason that she and her family live on the husband's salary. However, her role as the sustenance of the family equals the husband's role of procuring the capital to sustain their daily lives. Both roles are critical to the survival of the family unit. Although the roles differ, it is certainly inappropriate to call a housewife dependent. The husband and wife are mutually dependent—the two together are economically independent in the larger sense. This new concept is readily gaining currency in Japanese families.

4

QUALITY CONTROL
OF HUMAN RESOURCES

In recent years, many business managers, union leaders, and journalists from the United States, Western Europe, and other countries have visited Japan one after another to study Japan's high productivity. Such a phenomenon could not have been imagined a decade ago. Devoting themselves to the task of "learning from Japan," these visitors sought to uncover the secret behind Japan's high productivity and the superior quality of its goods. After the observation tours, most of them came to the conclusion that Japan's success was due to its group-oriented dynamics, which mobilizes the enthusiasm and cooperation of workers, and to its effective application of quality control techniques in production. Above all, these visitors felt that the total quality control (TQC) program was the true secret behind Japan's high-quality goods. Their conclusion is not wrong, but it is only part of the story, for these technically minded visitors focused solely on the production systems.

It is true that modern production techniques have contributed significantly to the growth of Japanese industries. The total quality control program, in particular, which developed from statistical quality control, has greatly contributed to the superior quality of Japanese products. The effectiveness of QC circles in

Japanese factories is indisputable, and the QC activities have resulted in tremendous improvement in the production process.

Nevertheless, technical superiority is not the real secret behind Japan's high productivity. If sophisticated technology alone ensured victory in economic competition, Japan would be far behind the countries from which it has imported most of the technologies. Japan's success, if it is to be called a success, has stemmed, not from the equipment, facilities, and technologies at the plants, but rather from the effective utilization of human resources in industry. Even in quality control, another imported technique, it is the workers' strong desire to produce superior goods at each level of production that has realized the high quality of Japanese products. The real key has been the "consciousness raising" of workers on the whole.

Some years ago, campaigns carried out at a large plant to improve quality and productivity created a serious labor problem. The cases were brought before the Diet and were condemned as an inhuman "efficiency first" movement by the labor union. At present, however, the General Council of Trade Unions of Japan (Sohyo) and other labor federations approve the QC activities, as long as they remain within the framework of the Labor Standards Act. They say, "What is important for the workers is how such activities are carried out. The quality circles, at present, are led by workers and pose no problem between labor and management." In the United States, most quality control campaigns are carried out under the guidance of management, but in Japan they are conducted by the workers themselves, who therefore can be regarded as participating members of management. The QC movement among workers is often called *jishu-kanri* (self-controlled activities), a concept that is now being exported and copied by many foreign industries. What is called "Japan's treasure" by the Japanese government is this self-controlled consciousness of workers. Japanese industries have been more successful in instilling among workers the highly automated desire to accomplish the jobs than in installing the quality control system in production lines.

Principles of business administration or production techniques are not absolute; they are affected by the culture of the society. The vigor of Japanese industry stems from the effective management of human resources. The successful quality control of human emotions, based on two traditional concepts of Japanese culture—duty and dependence—is the true secret behind Japan's productivity. In this chapter, therefore, I will try to demonstrate how Japanese management conducts its unique quality control system.

In order to introduce the total picture, I direct your attention to Figure 5. While referring to it, I shall explain each box in detail so you can fully understand the total quality control system.

Paternalism—Philosophy of Japanese Management

As pointed out in Chapter 1, Japan is an economic latecomer. The Japanese company system as we know it today emerged only in the Meiji era—late in the nineteenth century. Craft shops, with paternalistic masters and their apprentices and journeymen, are out of date now, but they are the forerunners of the small "underdeveloped" factories of today. The owner-manager of a small factory plays the double role of father and employer, and the workers behave like members of the company family rather than as mere employees. The relationship between workers and management, in a way, resembles that of a fraternal order in which all are fate-sharing members of the same group. An employer usually looks upon his employees as a father does his children; and a good foreman looks upon his workers as a brother does his younger brothers. The company's activities and programs penetrate the life of each worker far beyond the daily work situation. Such problems as family finances, housing, and the

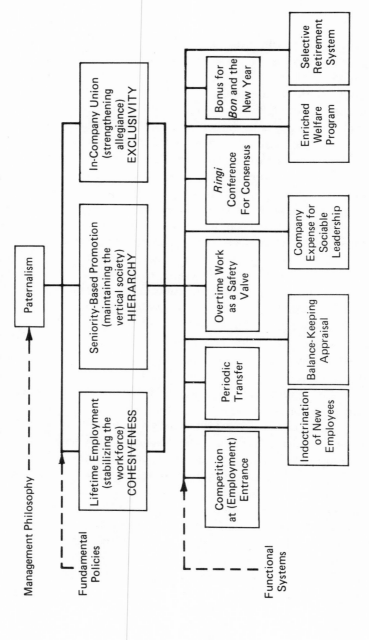

Figure 5. Quality control of human resources in Japan.

education of children are usually within the scope of the company's activities. What is most notable about the system is that the company's role is not taken reluctantly or accepted grudgingly. Both management and workers assume that it is the father's—management's—responsibility to involve himself in such matters, and the children's—the workers'—privilege to receive such care and attention. It is a familylike arrangement.

In larger firms, the relationship between management and workers is definitely more remote and impersonal, since management can hardly duplicate the small owner-manager's paternal and intimate knowledge of the workers. Yet even here there is a matrix of obligation and responsibility that holds all members together. When a worker enters a large company, he is committing his entire life to the organization. In return, the company is held responsible for his economic livelihood. Even an incompetent or inefficient member of the group is cared for; he is given an appropriate place and is not expelled from the group. However, the arrangement is more clanlike than familylike, since the company is so large. The president is much like a feudalistic *daimyō* (lord); the workers are samurai vassals; and the company as a whole is the clan of the Tokugawa period. The workers' cohesion and sense of belonging are very similar to the loyalty and devotion of vassals in feudal days.

In short, the central force used by Japanese management to drive human resources is paternalism. The basic attitude of employers in Japan is parental—to let employees depend childishly *(amaeru)* on management—and employees accordingly are inclined to depend *(amaetagaru)* on management. The verb *amaeru* is derived from the adjective *amai*, which literally means "sweet," in the sense of a sweet taste, but is figuratively used to describe self-indulgent behavior in a situation where there is some special relationship between two people or groups. It can be said that Japanese management is *amai* to employees and that employees *amaeru* on management.

In the contract society of the West, a new worker is given a job description which tells him what he is to do and how he is to behave at work. Although he receives supervision from his boss, he is fundamentally left to himself. The whole situation tells him, "Help yourself," much as if he had been invited to a feast. He has to accomplish his job by himself, according to the job description. He is free to do his own work, but at the same time he cannot expect help from others. There is an atmosphere of "Nobody else will help you!" The relationship between employer and employee is usually set off by the exchange of labor (contribution) and wages (reward). Therefore the relationship is not vertical but rather horizontal.

In Japan, a worker is employed not by written contract but by unwritten law—a law for all family members. The worker receives a written appointment paper stating his starting salary and a booklet on company regulations. The paper is not a contract but rather the announcement of the co-relationship. When he is placed in a certain work group, he is not given any job description but is usually told, "We will help you. Depend on us!" Appropriate work is assigned to him as proof that he has become a new member of the group. The entire workload is accomplished by all members in cooperation. Thus the relationship between employer and employee is based on the feudal concept of *on* (a psychological debt of gratitude).

There is a saying in Japanese: "A man incurs *on* even through a single night's stay." As this suggests, *on* implies the receiving of some kindness, along with the psychological burden of repaying the kindness in some way. Employment is a favor of the employer to the employee, as it was that of the lord to his samurai, and the employee is indebted for the favor. Therefore, the employee pledges himself to the *on* provided by the employer. The worker repays the debt by dedicating himself to the work, much as a samurai devoted himself to his lord. But the *on* is so profoundly abstract and difficult to quantify that it is almost impossible to repay. Accordingly, the dedicated efforts of workers to repay *on* become rather endless.

The relationship between employer and employee is always vertical. It continues after working hours and even extends beyond retirement. However, no one can deny that there is a contractual aspect to the relationship, even though no contract is written on paper. Some scholars refer to such Japanese groups as the "kin-tract" society (a combination of "kinship" and "contract"), a term originated by psychologist Francis L. K. Hsu. But I have coined the term "*on*-tract" society, because *on* is very often the prime mover in driving people to reach a contractual agreement and to fulfill the mutual obligations created by the relationship.

The ideology of paternalism instills a strong sense of belonging in the minds of workers. The employees, in turn, like good children or loyal subordinates of *daimyō*, willingly follow what the company desires. Of course, the Japanese people are intelligent and do not blindly follow or swallow anything offered by management; but they do enjoy the exclusive atmosphere of their own work group as all members join together to achieve business success. This group-centered enthusiasm is the most important consequence of the paternalistic system.

The scientific management movement established by Frederick W. Taylor emphasized the use of money to make a man work. Since human beings need money to survive, it is truly a great motivator. Nevertheless, too much reliance on money to motivate people spoils them, and even begins to work on them like a drug. The more money people get, the more they want for their work. This is particularly true of workers who do not derive satisfaction from the work itself. Their addiction to money will increase year after year, and indiscriminate use of the drug will ruin their minds, if not their bodies.

Japanese management has never relied too much on money to motivate workers. They know that money can be used to move an item, but it is extremely difficult to move a man around with money. Of course, a man can be moved physically by money—such as paying a worker a premium to transfer from a head office to a branch office. But unless the worker is fully convinced that his transfer is the right action for both himself and the company, his *mind* is not really moved from one place to the other. To move people's minds, Japanese employers know that they cannot depend solely on monetary rewards. This is the theory behind paternalistic management.

This paternalism, the central motivating force of management, is based on three policies, or pillars of the organization: lifetime employment, seniority-based promotion, and the in-company union. We will look into each of these features.

Lifetime Employment (Cohesiveness)

Today a "Safety First" sign is found on factory walls all over the world. This motto was started in America. Many years ago the management of an American factory proposed "Efficiency First" as a slogan to increase the productivity of its workers. The result was quite negative. With such high pressure placed on the workers to increase efficiency, accidents occurred frequently and productivity decreased. After that, management became aware that safety was the key to efficiency. Accordingly, the company established "Safety First" as its motto, and this spread all over the world.

Some Japanese managers were a little bit wiser and went one step further. They established "Safety First" as a motto not only for the factory operation but for the life of a worker as well. They offered the worker total job security. This meant, of course, "no firing" of employees. Thus the idea of lifetime employment was introduced in the Taisho era (1912–1926). At that time, the life expectancy of a Japanese male was around 44 years of age, so the guarantee of a job until retirement was really lifetime employment. Now Japanese men live an average of 73 years, so the term "lifetime employment" really refers to employment until retirement (usually between ages 55 and 60).

Late in the Meiji era (1868–1912) and early in the Taisho era, the turnover of blue-collar workers was quite high in Japan, and management suffered as a result. The timely introduction of "lifetime employment" improved the consciousness of workers and reduced the rate of turnover in the factories. This new practice gradually became the standard for the nation—the proverbial Japanese system. It gained widespread acceptance because it matched the cultural traditions of Japanese society. In the feudal society of the Tokugawa era, it was a disgrace for samurai to abandon the lord they served. (This was not true before the Tokugawa period, in the fifteenth and sixteenth centuries. It was then quite common for a samurai to turn his back on a weaker lord and join a stronger one or a more generous one who rewarded him better.) Tokugawa shoguns stressed such Confucian teachings as "A loyal samurai will not take a second lord" (*Chushin wa nikun ni mamiezu*) and "A faithful wife will not marry two times" (*Seppu wa nifu ni tsukaezu*). Thus singlehearted faithfulness became a virtue.

Since its introduction in the Taisho era, this unique employment style has taken firm root in Japanese industrial society. The system, which is almost inviolable, makes the work group the most cohesive group in a person's life. After finishing school, a new employee joins the group. He will always remain with the organization and will personally identify with the social level, reputation, progress, and success of the company. If his company is large and enjoys a solid reputation in the community, he himself is also considered great and is given high social status. In return for being looked after and protected, he renders dedicated service and gives complete loyalty to the company. He does not think of his relationship with the company in contractual terms, as is usual in the West. Like a vassal to the lord, he belongs wholeheartedly to the organization, to which by far the most valuable part of his life will be devoted.

In the West, the possibility of a worker quitting in a desire for advancement and the prerogative of the company to fire a worker are constant factors in the employer-employee relationship. Japanese companies, however, are reluctant to discharge employees because of a fear of destroying their long-established unity, and workers are reluctant to quit because of their "safety" status as lifetime employees. In 1974, right after the first oil crisis, the famous Japanese manufacturer Matsushita Electric suffered from the tremendous drop in sales of color TVs. Despite the production cut, the stocks continued to increase. The president decided to discharge some 10,000 workers. But Konosuke Matsushita, founder of the company, strongly opposed the move. "The workers are treasures. Never discharge them," he said. So the company adopted the *han-don* (half-day) system, an idea created by Matsushita himself during the recession of the 1930s. Production workers put in only half a day in the company, then spent the remaining half day out selling the stocks. The union was so pleased with the idea that it formed the "Sales Volunteer Force" on its own. The workers wiped out all the stocks in six months and returned to normal operation.

If a company discharges a worker unreasonably, or a worker terminates such a permanent relationship by what is thought to be his own selfish demand, the society as a whole attaches a particular stigma to the event. The company will lose its reputation and will have difficulty recruiting bright graduates from good schools. The worker will have a very hard time finding a good, stable job with any reputable company other than a foreign (non-Japanese) one. Unless he is remarkably talented, he is likely to become a refugee in the Japanese labor market.

The relationship between the company and the worker is not simply a function of the economic convenience of the two parties. The worker, whether a laborer or a manager, may not leave the company at his convenience for another position even if the departure is to his economic advantage. He is bound by *on* to remain in the company group. Loyalty to the group, with an interchange of responsibilities—a system of shared obligation—is the basis of employment. This system goes considerably beyond the written regulations and the Labor Standards Act which officially govern the industrial society.

Lifetime employment offers many advantages to the company. For one thing, it guarantees a steady labor force, which the company can then educate on a long-range plan and, more important, receive a benefit from that education in return. In order to cast workers in the right mold and achieve the desired quality, management brings in large batches of untrained graduates from high schools and universities each year rather than picking up trained people in the marketplace for specific jobs. These fresh workers are then indoctrinated to be loyal company members and are given the necessary training on the job and off the job throughout their careers. When a man stays with one company, he naturally becomes well accustomed to his job, learns to value it highly, and becomes well versed in company activities. Generally speaking, every member gets to be a kind of expert on company operations.

Of course, there are disadvantages as well. The most troublesome is that management almost always has to maintain a surplus labor force, since it is impossible to keep all employees up to date on the rapid economic and technological changes of the world. Inefficient use of the time and energy of these surplus workers is inevitable and leads to a conservative attitude toward rapid change on the part of the workers.

In order to reduce the surplus labor force, management will often transfer workers to its subcontracting firms or subsidiary companies. But in acute cases, such as the oil crises in the past, it asks for volunteers to leave the company. Temporary layoffs can be conducted only in the form of "volunteering," with the payment of a special dismissal allowance. However, there is a danger that the better workers will volunteer to leave and that the incompetent ones, who cannot get jobs easily, will prefer to stay on. Thus the success of personnel management under the lifetime employment system largely depends on how the company can manage redundancy.

First of all, the selection of employees at entrance must be carried out very carefully. Errors should be minimized in every way. Overtime work is required rather regularly in smaller firms, for it works as a buffer to the fluctuating workload. Temporary workers, part-timers, and *arubaito* (a term derived from the German word "Arbeit," indicating the lowest status of temporary workers in Japan), are employed in the regular work schedule but not treated as lifetime employees. All in all, personnel management is so elaborate as to strengthen the strong points and cover the weak points of the system. These are described in detail later in the chapter.

Seniority-Based Promotion (Hierarchy)

The lifetime employment system would not be so successful if it did not have a strong partner to sustain it. This partner has been the seniority-based promotion system.

Since Japanese people are so group-oriented, they are eager to be on a par with others. All workers are employed on "*on*-tract" terms, so they would not be happy if they were unreasonably differentiated in rewards. They do not consider their contributions to be rewarded solely in proportion to their ability and performance—the contractual terms of the West. Rather, loyalty is their most important offering and is given highest value by the society.

However, management needed to find some way to make

ranks in wages and status in order to maintain the vertical society. So it chose one indisputable criterion: age. The wage and salary administration program was operated by age difference, which is also, conceivably, equivalent to length of service under the system of lifetime employment. Management found this to be the best way to maintain harmony *(wa)* among the workforce, because nobody could complain about his age.

It is almost impossible to assess an individual's ability and performance in the Japanese workplace, since no job standard is allocated to a worker and the work is done by group hands. Nevertheless, to be fair to employees, management needed to consider the competence of individual workers in making its assessment, so it adopted another objective criterion: the level of education of each employee. The education of a worker is, in a way, a rough indication of his ability. The starting salaries of high school and university graduates are different even if the workers are placed initially in the same jobs. Also, the graduates of first-rate universities are ranked higher than graduates of second-rate universities. Therefore, the competitive society is now called the "credential" society. People need university credentials to enter the industrial world and move up in the pyramid. Thus the seniority system is now operated on three criteria: age, length of service, and school credentials.

People may enter a business firm or government service at different posts leading to different careers, but each career consists of a sort of age escalator of pay and status on which workers advance together. Blue-collar workers, for example, are on a relatively low escalator of pay and status, while white-collar elites who have qualified by higher education and a competitive entrance examination are on a high escalator that may lead all the way to executive posts. Even so, within each category, status as well as pay is determined primarily by age and length of service.

This seniority system supports lifetime employment, because it rewards workers according to their length of stay in the company. Generally, as a worker grows older he needs more money to maintain his livelihood, so to obtain a higher wage he stays longer with the company. The longer the worker extends his service, the more effective the lifetime employment system becomes. By the same token, lifetime employment reinforces the seniority system in that it regulates the hierarchical order of the organizational pyramid and satisfies the worker's need to feel equal with others. Both systems are much like the two wheels of a cart: each cannot run without the other. This combination is an extremely effective means of utilizing human resources by voluntary commitment rather than by constraint. With the security offered by lifetime employment and the benefits that accrue to the worker more or less automatically through the seniority system, Japanese industry has been able to retain the loyalty and energetic service of its employees and to pacify the unions in a way envied by the West.

There are, of course, weak points in the seniority system too. During the 1960s, when Japanese industry was achieving rapid economic development and was continuing to expand, it faced a critical shortage of fresh young workers to aid in its growth. Companies went into fierce competition to secure new workers. As a result, every company tried to offer attractive terms to the younger generation, and the starting salaries of new workers rose year after year. As already pointed out, the pay scale in the seniority system is set up in a hierarchical order which matches the pyramidal structure of the organization itself. When salaries and wages are increased at the bottom, the whole pay scale is automatically augmented. This imposes a heavy burden on the company finances, but the personnel expenditure can be covered as long as economic expansion is achieved and productivity continues to rise. With the sudden oil crisis, however, Japan's economic development was stunted and salaries and wages threatened to outstrip company revenues. As a result, companies had to devise some way to lay off employees.

Whenever temporary layoffs are made in the West, younger employees are eliminated first. That is what is meant by seniority. During the oil crisis, Japanese companies invited employees to volunteer for retirement by compensating them for early withdrawal from the lifetime employment system. Senior employees were asked to leave the company first, simply because they were imposing a greater financial burden on the organization. With this development, the seniority system lost much of its value for employees, since it no longer protected the senior members of the group. On the other hand, companies would have gone bankrupt if they had stubbornly tried to preserve the traditional seniority system. How Japanese management will operate this crucial system for managing human resources is something to watch for in the future.

A more important, and disadvantageous, aspect of the seniority system is that management has to promote an employee to section chief or an equivalent position simply by virtue of his having completed a certain length of service. In large business firms as well as government offices, age groups reinforce the hierarchy of rank, and those who entered together in any one year from the same graduating class will move in parallel in both salary and rank throughout most of their careers. Management is obligated to promote employees of the same "class" by any means, if not at the same time, before the next class is moved up.

As a result, it is not unusual for management to place an older employee in a managerial or equivalent position even if he is not really competent for the post. In such a case, management always finds a capable assistant to compensate for the incompetence of the manager. For the person selected as assistant, it is certainly a fine opportunity to obtain a promissory note for an executive post in the future. Those higher on the career escalator are seen merely as elders who got on the escalator earlier, not as workers who climbed up by ability to the higher posts. Almost everyone can be certain that his time will ripen in due course. In this manner, the Japanese hierarchy maintains *wa* (harmony) and breeds less tension and resentment than does the status-based system of the West.

In-Company Union (Exclusivity)

The following incident took place quite a while ago, but since the situation reflected still exists, it bears relating here.

The Japanese Shipbuilders Union invited representatives of the Trade Union Congress of Britain to inspect Japanese working conditions. The British delegates inspected all the major ship-building centers, from Hokkaido Island in the north to Kyushu Island in the south. Afterward, they returned to Tokyo and presented their findings at the branch office of the International Labor Organization. The leader of the British delegation, who spoke first, made this comment: "There is no union in Japan." Every Japanese attendee thought that he was joking, but it was not a joke. He continued, "When someone who has been working at your side is discharged and moves to another company, he immediately loses his union membership. That is not a union. People work together in the same factory doing the same work, but out of this workforce, a small group employed as temporary helpers is not allowed to belong to the union. That is not a union." He gave more examples, all to demonstrate that there was no union in Japan.

A certain blame may have to be placed on the ambiguity of such Japanese terms as "lifetime employment," which is so vague as to allow Japanese management to pay monthly dues to workers for their entire life and to call something quite unlike a union, a union. But the main problem is that the Japanese, with their tight-knit groups standing apart in the vertical society, recognize no common ground. They have a very strong and narrow-minded in-group orientation. Therefore, workers at one company are not likely to unite with workers from rival companies to raise wage scales or improve working conditions. Instead, they would rather compete with rival workers to increase their own company's revenues (the source of wages)—much as samurai competed with enemy samurai to promote the good name of their lord and thus increase the stipend allotted to their fief. Japan remains a vertical society.

There are many labor federations in Japan, including the General Council of Trade Unions of Japan (Sohyo), the Japan Council of Metal Workers Unions (Zenkinzoku), and the Japanese Federation of Iron and Steelworkers Unions (Tekko-roren). These are the established common grounds for workers, designed to promote their horizontal relationships and communications and thus build an integrated labor movement. However, the workers do not feel any special responsibility to these groups. In general, their loyalty and sense of belonging reside with the company. The union is a secondary consideration for a worker, since he can hold union membership only as long as he stays with the company.

I understand that Western civilization has its roots in the tribes of horsemen, hunters, and herders who originally settled in Europe. In those early times, certain forests and pastures needed to be set aside as public grounds, since many tribes depended on those lands for their living. They knew that if they hunted too much in a forest, or grazed a pastureland down to the roots, they and others would lose their means of livelihood. They were adamant about not allowing others into their private holdings, but at the same time they felt a strong mutual responsibility to maintain public lands. The labor unions and trade unions of the West grew out of this strong feeling of mutual responsibility.

By contrast, the Japanese have been an agricultural people from earliest times. Rice fields were clearly marked off as the property of one house or village, and the people's livelihood was made by tending these fields. Though all village members shared water rights, and though they worked in close cooperation, they felt no ties of mutual responsibility to other villages. Outside their own village, they were free from the ties of *giri* (social duty) and *ninjō* (human feeling). This heritage perhaps explains why the Japanese do not have horizontal unions in the Western sense.

Japanese workers are organized not by crafts or trades but by companies. White-collar and blue-collar workers are all in one union. They have never felt any need to oppose technological progress or strategic change in their company by demanding featherbedding or the like, as their Western counterparts often do. They know that all the changes are made at the expense of the company. Furthermore, a union leader rarely opposes company policy. Far from being hostile, he usually makes demands in a spirit of cooperation with the company. There is good reason for this. He and other union members are on the same promotional escalator in the organization. Someday, as an executive, he may be in a position to receive union demands himself. While serving as a union leader, he looks ahead and thinks of his future role. Psychologically, he is already a member of management when he is elected union leader.

As a matter of fact, the union leader is in an advantageous position for climbing the promotional ladder. Capitalizing on his central position, in which he comes in contact with employees in various departments, he can establish close personal relationships with many people and thereby collect valuable information from every corner of the company. Needless to say, he can make good use of this information all the way up to the executive post. (In fact, there are many executives who used to be union leaders. Nikkeiren, the Japanese Federation of Employers' Associations, recently surveyed 534 large companies and discovered that 992 out of 6,121 executives, or 16.2 percent, had been influential union leaders.)

Few union leaders dare to spoil such an excellent opportunity by opposing the company unreasonably. Only a very small percentage of leaders have actively opposed their companies. They are the ones who have erred on the escalator up, or who grieve on a lower escalator because they are unable to reach their destination.

In Japan, the union's extremely soft attitude toward company demands is called *goyō kumiai* (a kept union, or a company union). The word *goyō* has its roots in the Tokugawa era, when the peasants, artisans, and merchants had to make a quick response to meet the demand *(goyō)* of the lord or his subordinate samurai. A popular scene in the samurai movies of today is a policeman carrying a lantern, painted with the letters *goyō*, chasing a criminal and trying to make him surrender by shouting, *"Goyō! Goyō!"*

Goyō is a demand from the upper echelons, but it is not restricted to a business sense. There are also expressions like *goyō tei* (an imperial villa), *goyō shonin* (a merchant under government patronage), *goyō shimbun* (a government-controlled press), *goyō terebi* (a government-controlled television broadcast), and *goyō kiki* (an order taker).

Competition at Employment Entrance

In Japan, a man begins his career with a company immediately after graduating from school, and the lifetime employment system requires him to stay with the company for 30 years or more. Therefore, entrance into a certain firm is the crucial beginning point of his career and really determines his life. Nothing could be more important for him, since it is an irreversible step. Indeed, even his marriage is likely to be determined by his social status— where he is employed.

On the other hand, it is also of serious importance for the company to hire fresh members each year on a permanent basis. Once workers have been hired, management cannot discharge them easily, so any errors in personnel selection take a considerable toll in organizational efficiency. It is estimated that ¥220 million (nearly $1 million) is spent on each employee during his stay with a company.

Almost all Japanese firms recruit new graduates in April of each year, because students leave school in March. Japanese management usually hires inexperienced workers, estimating individual potential on a long-term basis, whereas management in the West will recruit experienced workers for certain jobs.

Here is an example of the usual process in Japan: A company starts sending out its introductory brochure as early as January or February of, say, 1982 to the short list of students to be graduated from first-rate universities the following year. The brochure is intended to attract these undergraduates when hiring takes place in October and November for April of 1983. Only the brightest students are the target at this time of year. The undergraduates select their first and second choices, and perhaps third choices too. In accordance with the rules of the Ministry of Labor, from October 1 onward, students may make formal inquiry visits to firms. The companies can then officially start their recruitment for the coming year.

Further selection tests and interviews are scheduled for November, but excellent candidates are usually interviewed unofficially and secretly reserved by the companies before October. Such preliminary contact or active recruitment before October 1 is called *aotagari* (cropping while the rice field is still green) and is strictly banned by the Ministry of Labor. There have been times in the past when *aotagari* became rather fierce, interfering with the student's studies and creating havoc in the labor market. Any company that violates the recruitment rule by engaging in *aotagari* is publicized by the Ministry of Labor as a social punishment. Such a company is likely to lose its reputation and be handicapped for future recruitment.

Nonetheless, some companies do engage in *aotagari* behind

the scenes by having employees who are alumni of the best schools lure the brightest students over drinks and talk. Those candidates who make every company's mouth water are, of course, the top-notch students from a sharply limited number of universities who have won a victory over the notorious "examination hell." This group, which includes future high-ranking civil servants, comprises about 3 to 4 percent of the 300,000 new graduates each year.*

Approximately 250 firms are listed in the first stock market of Kabuto-cho (the Wall Street of Tokyo). These companies, which are considered large-scale, reliable businesses, scramble for the top-class students each year. The capability of every personnel manager is evaluated by the number of acquisitions he makes from this top-notch group. The companies acquiring none are not few. Students are polled by the press each year on the popularity of large firms, and 100 companies are listed in order of popularity in the leading newspapers. All the companies are eager to be listed in the higher ranks, so they can gain popularity and thus obtain better candidates for employment.

What is the marketability of new graduates in Japan? As shown in Figure 6, the top-class students are in the "seller's market." Below them is a layer of students in the "marginal market." There are not enough top-notch graduates to fill the requirements of the large firms, so those in the marginal layer have a chance to obtain the remaining openings. Students in the next layer, the "relative buyer's market," rarely get jobs in the large firms. However, they do have a slim chance, through nepotism and other paternalistic means.

For instance, the executive of a manufacturing firm might hire the son of a friend or relative if asked to do so. The friend or

---

*In 1982 the Ministry of Labor relinquished its control over *aotagari* because the practice had become so widespread behind the scenes. Ministry officials left the situation to a gentlemen's agreement between universities and the industrial society.

Figure 6. Marketability of new graduates.

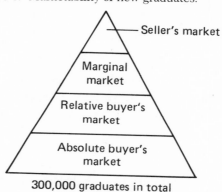

300,000 graduates in total

relative, in turn, may someday repay the *on* of the executive by arranging a position of some importance in another firm for a son or a nephew of the executive. Thus the son of a former president of an oil company can be employed by a large trading company even if he is in the "relative buyer's market." This happens quite often in the "*on*-tract" society, where personal relationships are so important. The practice may seem to contradict the philosophy behind lifetime employment, but it is not necessarily the case. First of all, this paternalistic type of employment ensures the loyalty and subservience of the employee, and potential problems are controlled to a large extent in advance. Second, a good personal connection bridges two companies and may enhance the business.

Those students at the bottom layer of the pyramid are in the "absolute buyer's market." They usually have to apply to smaller firms, where neither lifetime employment nor the seniority system really functions properly. They have to work hard, at lower salaries and for longer hours, because their companies are much more vulnerable to bankruptcy than the larger firms. These are the workers who have to depend on their own ability and performance. Accordingly, turnover is rather high in smaller companies.

Candidates from high schools are drawn from a wider geographical range than are university graduates. Since able students in the metropolitan areas usually go on to colleges and universities, candidates for employment from urban areas who have no college ambitions are seldom worth a company's consideration. Thus the future operational hands in the factory are recruited largely from nonurban high schools. The company usually asks high school teachers to recommend qualified candidates, or the principal of the school and the teachers approach the company to request that their students be considered for employment. Therefore, almost all candidacies are arranged by the teachers and recruitment proceeds as planned. Very few errors in selection have been reported.

Indoctrination of New Employees

The uniform quality of education provides Japanese industry with an excellent supply of generally competent workers who are prepared for and receptive to learning specialized skills in the workplace. Japanese firms, taking advantage of the lifetime employment pattern, can deploy a long-range plan to train these employees in specific skills and mold them into useful and governable human assets.

There are numerous programs for training company employees, including the Young Executive Development Program, the Middle Management Development Program, the Supervisory Development Program, the R&D Personal Development Program, the Sales Training Course, and the Skilled Workers Training Course. These are all similar to the training programs in other industrialized countries. But there is one unique program of Japanese management: The New Employees Orientation Program.

Many large and medium-size firms spend three to four months—sometimes even six months—indoctrinating fresh young workers who join the company in April of the cherry-blossom season each year. Newcomers are not assigned to any specific jobs during the orientation period. They are first briefed on the company's perspective and are taught about the particular business circle the company belongs to—for instance, the automobile world, the banking world, or the oil world. They then learn the organizational structure and all the functions of the company. After the briefing, they are assigned to offices and plants on a temporary placement scheme and are rotated at short intervals (one week at most) from section to section in these offices and plants. Each one of them is proud to wear the brand new gray company smock and enjoys being a migratory bird. Through this job rotation program, new workers learn the functional activities of the company and gain the companywide views. In each section, the chief and all other members who are superiors to a new employee welcome him and imbue him with a strong group spirit and a sense of the importance of conforming to precedents.

In addition, some companies do not hesitate to send their young recruits to the Self-Defense Force to inspire them with a militaristic rigor. Some even take them into a Zen temple for spiritual training in meditation. A few conduct a "training camp" program by keeping new employees in the company lodge or dormitory for a week or so. They sing the company song and get a briefing on the day's schedule each morning. They prepare meals and beds, do laundry, clean the premises, take lessons on business subjects, and do physical exercise. A few companies even take trainees to see a classic play like *Chushingura*.

The purpose of these special training programs is to transform the new employees into energetic, dedicated company workers. Japanese management strikes while the iron is hot—while the work habits of the newcomers are still unformed—and thus controls the quality of its human resources.

Periodic Transfer

New graduates from universities are not experienced or trained to assume management responsibility. At the same time, owing to their status when employed, they cannot be placed as floor workers in the plants. They are therefore developed under the long-range company plan and are usually assigned to a number of staff and administrative posts by the periodic transfer program. In this job-rotation program, selected white-collar employees are moved from one section to another every two or three years (three to four years in some companies). The program gives the employees an opportunity to become skilled in the various functions of the organization and to broaden their proficiency.

Japanese management shies away from creating specialists. In the lifetime employment system, specialists offer no flexibility to the organization and are usually kept to a minimum. Even in the plants, skilled workers are occasionally transferred within the various plant operations to learn new production skills. Traditionally, management has tended to create multipurpose generalists who can be at the company's disposal if any organizational change should be required to meet current economic conditions. By reshuffling these "utility players," Japanese industries have successfully reorganized the production lines and sales forces to overcome the two oil crises of the past.

In the vertical organization, everybody tries to move upward on the escalator and become *kachō* (section chief) or *buchō* (department head). The society pays much more respect to the title of *chō*, which means a man in charge of others, than to the title of a specific profession, like senior engineer or market researcher. Naturally, everyone wishes to train himself in the skills of various posts and have broad capabilities commensurate with a *chō* position. Thus the periodic transfer system meets the needs of both management and employees.

Each company has its own policy on transfers. In addition, employees themselves may request a transfer through the self-notification system. Annually or semiannually, every employee is given a chance to express his desire for career development on the self-notification form and to submit it to his designated chief. The chief and the subordinate discuss the matter in a counsel interview and examine possibilities for the employee's future development. The employee might express a desire to stay in the same section and keep on the same course. In any case, the transfer proposal will be presented to the personnel department for consideration.

Perhaps the greatest significance of the periodic transfer program is that it counterbalances the lifetime employment and seniority systems of Japanese organizations. If employees of one section or department were to stay with the same group for 30 years or more in the rigid hierarchy, they would almost certainly become bored and discouraged by their jobs. Morale would stagnate and conflicts might arise to destroy efficiency. Workers definitely need a change periodically. Misplacements, grievances, and interpersonal conflicts are all alleviated by the periodic transfer system. Some people are promoted. Others may be transferred. For some employees it is a mere horizontal transfer; for others, a demotion. The exact nature of the transfer is never clearly announced, but it becomes obvious sooner or later to everyone. These transfers usually take place in April—the season for personnel administration in Japan.

Most of the large and medium-size firms follow this system. Only a few of them transfer employees, out of necessity, other than periodically. The small firms do not have enough posts to rotate employees and do so only occasionally. All in all, the quality of employees is well controlled and balanced by this system.

Balance-Keeping Appraisal

In accordance with the seniority-based pay scales, everybody gets an increase in pay automatically each year. Since employees are grouped as members of an "annual class," their positions are also pushed up each year with the entry of new workers. There is little competition across age or status lines. In principle, a subordinate cannot leapfrog an incompetent superior, and the superior has no fear of challenge from an able and ambitious subordinate.

All this, again, is in principle. If the system were to operate as cited above, all older employees would automatically graduate into the "managerial" and "executive" ranks—in other words, everybody would eventually become *kachō* and *buchō*. However, there are fewer *kachō* positions than there are employees from the same annual class. The number of *buchō* positions is even lower, so all *kachō* cannot be promoted to *buchō* at the same time. Out of these few *buchō*, management executives are singled out.

In order to resolve this discrepancy in the seniority system, Japanese management has introduced the annual merit-rating system, in which, at least in theory, the individual is rated in relation to specific job demands and his accomplishments. However, in the typical Japanese plant or office, the job is done on a group basis and no one tries to demonstrate individual brilliance or dynamic leadership. It is therefore extremely difficult to isolate individual competence or job responsibility and to carry out a fair rating of each employee. Because of such difficulties, a leader tends to evaluate subordinates with small differentials in ratings. Not only work performance but attitude toward superiors, sociability, and other personal qualities are taken into account in the merit calculation in order to be fair to the employee. The halo effect may also influence the evaluation. In any case, large differentials in ratings are avoided, for they would cripple human relationships in the work group.

All the ratings are reported to the personnel department, and again, to eliminate any unfair report and maintain the *wa* of the company, the department tries on its own initiative to balance all the ratings within a small marginal range. As a result, unlike the Harvard or Stanford MBA who becomes a vice president after two or three years on the job, no Japanese worker can become a star.

Nevertheless, an employee should not discount that small differential in rating if he hopes to be *kachō* when his time comes. During his 15- to 17-year apprenticeship, he tries ceaselessly to accumulate those small point margins which will indicate that he is the one to be appointed *kachō* first, or next. To be in the "managerial" or "executive" category in Japan requires a great deal of patience, endless effort, and the steady display of individual competence. Any careless mistake, therefore, decreases a worker's merit-rating points and deters his progress. A blunder could be fatal to his career.

Mr. C was a promising member of a large firm. With his credentials from Tokyo University, he was appointed Chief of the Welfare Section when his annual "class" was considered for *kachō* positions. He climbed up the pyramid rapidly and seemed destined for an executive post. One day, as the head of employee welfare, he hired a carpentry service to repair the company apartment house. At the time, he and his family were living in the same housing unit, and his wife asked the carpenter to repair the doorknob of their apartment. Since it was a private order, his wife offered to pay the carpenter personally. The carpenter refused such a small payment because he wanted to please the Chief of the Welfare Section and be hired again by the company. So the wife did not pay for the work on the doorknob. Another housewife living in the same quarters learned of the incident and told her husband about it at the dinner table. The next day, he related the incident to another member of the company, and the story found its way to a certain company executive. It came out that the Chief of the Welfare Section had had his door repaired at company expense. Thus his merit-rating record was dealt a fatal blow. His one and only mistake (actually his wife's mistake) spoiled his rosy future. For 15 years he remained *kachō* in an unimportant corner of the company while some of his comrades in the same annual class rose to *buchō*.

In summary, to prevent possible complaints and maintain the Japanese sense of egalitarianism, a company makes only a small marginal differential in rating each employee. At the same time, for the purpose of screening candidates for managerial positions, it takes considerable points away from the employee who has made obvious mistakes. Management is really undertaking an awesome task in trying to maintain harmony among its employees.

Overtime Work as a Safety Valve

One of the most widely held beliefs is that the Japanese work harder than Americans or Europeans, but the observation should be made with some caution. It would not be accurate to draw this conclusion solely on the basis of total hours worked without taking into account the density of work and the reason that Japanese workers remain longer in the workplace.

In opposition to the general principle that overtime work is required to meet urgent production needs, many Japanese factories call for overtime work regularly and pay workers a premium for it. This premium comprises a considerable portion of the workers' income. The reasoning behind this unusual practice is that management needs the overtime work schedule as a buffer in order to manage the fluctuating workload with the minimum labor force it maintains under the lifetime employment system. To bridge the gap between an inflexible workforce and fluctuating business conditions, management also uses temporary workers, part-timers, and subcontractors. However, these workers are not up to the standard of their own experienced employees and are not always reliable. Therefore, the flexible overtime work schedule is the best way to maintain the desired productivity and keep up with swings in the business cycle. Thus workers receive an overtime work allowance as a portion of their regular income, though it fluctuates a bit on the wave of the company's business dealings.

Looking at the widely used subcontracting system in Japan, we see that the overtime work schedule is an important safety valve in meeting the inflow of work from a parent company. Work orders are issued irregularly from the parent company and are distributed through secondary and tertiary subcontractors, or even further down the line. (See Figure 7.) The further the orders are distributed, apportioned in smaller pieces, the more

Figure 7. The subcontracting system.

Delivery is made successively upward

Parent Company

Primary Subcontractor

Secondary Subcontractor

Tertiary Subcontractor

Work is apportioned downward

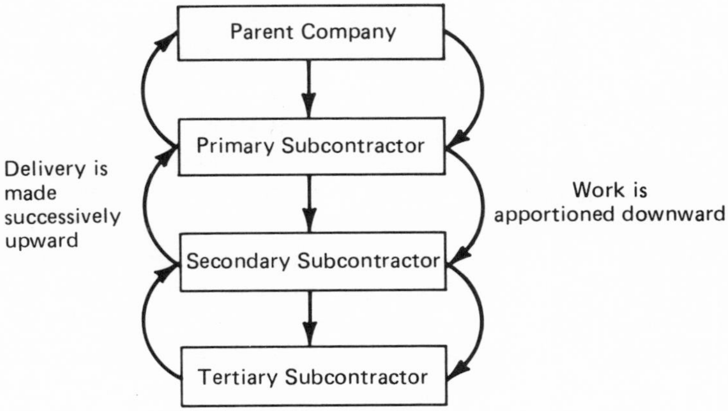

rigidly the delivery date is fixed and the tighter the production schedule becomes. The delivery date has to be met by any possible means and the subcontractors have to work intensively for a short period.

Overtime work is essential for the subcontractors. This is not to say that the workers are always kept busy during their regular working hours. In fact, in the lower subcontracting firms, workers are often idle during the regular hours and busy in the overtime hours. This is the main reason why base pay is deceptively low in the smaller companies; the workers earn their sustenance through the overtime work allowance. Thus, for the workers as well as management, the overtime schedule is an absolute necessity, and this safety valve functions well in the Japanese organization.

White-collar workers too put in long hours, but often away from the job. For instance, at the lunch table, over drinks on the way home, and on the golf course on Sundays, they are fond of discussing matters related to their work. This does not mean that the Japanese are, to use the word now in vogue, "workaholics." Devotion to the job is part of their samurai tradition. In the Tokugawa period, samurai were supposed to be on "24-hour standby," ever ready to devote themselves to the lord of their fief.

The willingness of the Japanese people to work longer hours also derives from the tradition of an agricultural race. In the farming society, particularly in the earlier days, working from dawn to late evening in the rice paddy and the fields was commonplace. The pattern remained unchanged for centuries. The people enjoyed staying in the fields while taking intermittent rests and chatting with each other. This work habit has been inherited by the modern Japanese businessman. The density of work is far different from that of Western workers, who concentrate on the work like lions, filling their empty stomachs one day and spending the next three days on an easy, sleepy vacation in the forests.

Company Expenses for Sociable Leadership

The statement that "a good *kachō* or *buchō* looks upon his subordinates as a father does his children" would receive almost unanimous agreement among Japanese employees, though it might meet with strong distaste in America and Europe. Such a superior-subordinate relationship fosters teamwork by offering workers paternalistic guidance in accomplishing the work.

The paternalistic organization obviously requires a considerable degree of close understanding between manager and subordinate, because in the seniority-based promotion system job competence is not a main factor and does not necessarily figure into the leadership equation. Japanese managers are not expected to be tough, forceful, and dynamic like their Western counterparts. Rather, the quality of a leader is usually evaluated in terms of his warmth and sensitivity. The manager inspires admiration and confidence among his subordinates more through his paternalistic behavior than through the sharpness of his professional views or his vigorous guidance on the job. What the Westerner might consider a desirably strong leadership quality—say, the ability to get the job done quickly—would cause resentment in Japan. Consensus through consultation is the norm for a Japanese leader.

Subordinates are lifetime members of a clan-type organization, and they expect to be treated as junior associates or even younger brothers rather than as mere underlings who prepare the groundwork for the seniors. In turn, the manager prefers subordinates who are loyal, obedient, and submissive, because the work of the section or the department and its progress are dependent in large measure on personal and noneconomic factors. The close superior-subordinate relationship plays a large part in the quality of group work.

To enhance this relationship, the manager occasionally invites his subordinates to a bar or tavern. There, they relax in an informal atmosphere and enjoy intimate conversation over drinks. Through this informal exchange of views, they cultivate mutual understanding, and through his hierarchical treat (the superior pays the bill) the manager strengthens his leadership. This is commonplace in the "*on*-tract" society. In return for the manager's favor *(on)* subordinates have a psychological debt to work harder to repay the *on* on the job.

However, frequent treats would place a considerable financial burden on the manager, even though they strenghtened his standing. So the company—the paternalistic guardian—has come to sponsor a leader's official sociabilities.

There are no reliable statistics on drinks at company expense, but from the results of some limited questionnaire surveys, I would like to summarize the current trend:

• Approximately 70 percent of all *kachō* are officially allotted a social expense account by the company. (All *buchō* have such an expense budget.)
• The remaining 30 percent of *kachō* receive no allowance for social activities. But of this percentage, (1) some *kachō* are given an allotment for the section as a whole (the budget for the section is at the *kachō*'s discretion), and (2) some *kachō* have an unofficial expense budget granted by tacit consent.

The monthly allotments for social expenses, and the percentage of managers in each category, are listed below:

As needed	20%
¥200,000–500,000	15%
¥100,000–200,000	20%
¥ 50,000–100,000	9%
¥ 30,000– 50,000	12%
Less than ¥30,000	12%
Confidential	9%
More than ¥1 million	3%

(The reader may convert these amounts into dollars roughly at the rate of ¥220 to $1, or whatever is currently appropriate.)

The above-listed amounts include all sorts of social expenses, but it is well known that *kachō* spend some portion of the allotment to enhance the superior-subordinate relationship. Those who enjoy an active social life at company expense are called *shayōzoku* (the company-expense tribe). At taverns and bars they engage in amusing conversation with business associates and with the bar hostesses, who skillfully flatter their male egos and provide an exclusive atmosphere for them. The press recently reported that in 1980 the total expenditure of *shayōzoku* was around ¥290 billion.

Ringi Conference for Consensus

Yokini hakarae is a samurai expression used exclusively by clan lords in the Tokugawa era. It means "Do with it as you see fit," or "Process it to the best of your knowledge and capability." As the expression suggests, a good lord never tried to stick his nose into small administrative matters. He took part only in decision making of utmost importance concerning the management of his fief, and left everything else to his subordinate samurai, saying, "*Yokini hakarae*."

This feudal pattern has given rise to the Japanese bottom-up administration, called the *ringi* system. *Ringi* literally means a circulation conference, and well over 90% of all large Japanese companies and many small ones follow this decision-making pattern. Government agencies also follow it. The system is based on the principle that any corporate decision should be made by a consensus of members concerned, instead of being made in dictatorial fashion. Important proposals relating to business management are drafted by the person responsible for the subject at the bottom of the organizational pyramid. By frequently consulting his immediate superior, he drafts the *ringi* paper—a sort of buck slip known as *ringisho*—which is then circulated upward and horizontally among all sections or departments concerned.

Each person who receives the *ringisho* is expected to study the proposal and affix his seal *(hanko)* to it as a sign that he has seen the document and does not actively oppose it. A person who intends to oppose or revise the proposal usually telephones the originator and expresses his disagreement. His negative reaction may be taken up in other conferences and may kill the proposal. To avoid such a negative reaction during circulation of the *ringisho,* the originator lays the groundwork beforehand in an effort to obtain the verbal agreement of those concerned. If this preparatory groundwork *(nemawashi)* is not done carefully, somebody may try to block the proposal by pigeonholing the *ringisho* for a while or someone may show his objection by affixing his seal upside down. Others may pass the buck by stamping their seal sideways, which signifies that they do not wish to be held responsible for the proposal.

Nemawashi is gardener's jargon in Japan. Literally, it means binding and protecting the roots of a tree before transplanting it. When the tree is chosen for transplanting, the gardener first digs around it, cutting off the smaller roots in the ground and trimming the branches to maintain a balance between roots and branches. Then the tree is dug out and the root ball is wrapped with a straw mat. The uprooted tree is then placed in the shade for a few days in order to let it adjust its physical conditions for the coming trip to the new soil. Only afterward is the tree transplanted in a new location. Similarly, in a business organization, a "subject tree" should be planted only after a careful *nemawashi* has been done. Only then does the proposal have a chance of getting through.

The *ringi* system itself is a form of *nemawashi* designed to obtain official consensus on a proposal which is then laid before top management. Yet it needs a sort of preliminary *nemawashi* to pave the way for circulation of the *ringisho*. This leads to quite a delay in decision making, and the delay can be fatal in times of fluctuating economic conditions. In some companies, therefore, "urgent" is stamped on special proposals to speed up the process. Other companies have a special procedure allowing urgent proposals to bypass certain sections. Some bypassed controversial points are directly brought into the executive committee meetings attended by the president, vice president, and other directors and are freely discussed there.

At any rate, when the *ringisho* finally reaches the top, the decision is made—adoption, approval, or rejection. Confirmation of the decision means that companywide consensus has been attained and implementation proceeds rapidly. It is silly for anyone to try to oppose the consensus at this stage, for unilateral disapproval offends the Japanese group spirit. The only alternative is to cooperate and assist in implementing the project. All staff members who affixed their seals on the proposal, from all departments or sections involved, are responsible for implementation.

The fact that the *ringisho* originates from fairly low down in the organization might suggest that top management is relinquishing some of its authority. But this is not really the case. A proposal is often conceived by the president, his directors, or his department heads, and is then hinted to the section specifically responsible for the matter. The task of drawing up and documenting the proposal is usually referred to someone at the bottom level. In the West, by contrast, a considerable proportion of management ideas are conceived in the executive suite and then imposed from the top down. The distinctive Japanese system of decision making, therefore, has numerous merits even though it takes so much time to reach a consensus. Specifically:

- It has the same effect as decentralized control.
- The circulation of the *ringisho* improves internal communication.

- The *ringisho,* as a circular, serves a reporting function.
- The *ringisho* is a kind of preconceived implementation plan, and has the effect of confirming implementation.
- The *ringi* system stimulates the initiative of people at the bottom level and utilizes their abilities. It makes everybody feel like a member of the management team. This is an excellent motivator.

Enriched Welfare Program

It was common in the Tokugawa era for a *daimyō* (feudal lord) to set up a residential district for his vassals and to have all of them live around his castle. The houses for these samurai were financed by the clan, and the size of a samurai's house was determined by his hierarchical status, with *karō* (the senior executive rank) living in a grand mansion and *ashigaru* (the lowest samurai rank) living in a tenement apartment. The samurai residential area was clearly set apart from the town, where artisans and merchants made their daily living.

One of the remaining evidences of this arrangement is the city of Fukuoka on Kyushu Island. This horizontally stretched-out city along Hakata Bay is divided by the beautiful Nakagawa River. The west bank of the river is the Fukuoka area, where the residence of samurai (vassals of the Kuroda clan) were located, and the east bank is the town of Hakata, where the feudal masses once bustled around the streets. Both names are still used to identify the area. The city itself is officially called Fukuoka, and the ruins of the lord's castle and moat are found in the west side of the city. But its national railroad station bears the name Hakata, since it is situated in the east. Thus any traveler wishing to visit the city by train has to purchase a ticket for Hakata Station.

Similar housing arrangements exist in Japan's present industrial society. Most large Japanese firms provide company-built and -subsidized housing for at least a third of their workforce. A company's housing quarters are customarily set apart from private residences in the area. All residents of such quarters are company employees and their families.

In addition, many firms have a loan system to assist employees in purchasing their own houses. According to a recent questionnaire survey of 818 companies conducted by the Ministry of Construction, the average company loan to an employee is ¥6,720,000 (approximately $30,000). The loaned amounts are repaid by installments deducted from the employee's monthly salary and semiannual bonuses, with the balance taken from his retirement allowance. The interest rate on the loan averages 4 to 6 percent. With the benefits of such a system, it is natural that workers are not eager to leave the company.

In-company savings accounts are also available to employees and offer a generous interest rate of 8 percent or more, which is definitely higher than the normal bank rate. Many a company holds an athletic meet annually for employees and their family members, and some seasonal festivities like a New Year celebration or a cherry-blossom party are held by the entire group or division at company expense. The Labor Standard Research Institute recently revealed that almost 90 percent of all Japanese firms, large and small, sponsor recreational company tours in spring and autumn. Many, if not all, firms maintain mountain lodges and seaside villas for their employees. Special commodities are supplied to employees at a discount price. The commuter fares are subsidized by the company. Tickets to concerts and plays are also available at a discount through the company. It seems that the company is more responsive to people's welfare than the government is, and leaves nothing to be desired. Employees, therefore, tend to lead their lives at the company's pace and schedule.

A few large trading companies have even devised a plan to

pay employees a generous pension during their postretirement years until they pass away. Toyota Auto Industry and its union have established the Toyota Welfare Fund, with assets of ¥4.5 billion (approximately $22 million), contributed largely from management, some from the union, and a little from each union member. The operating profits from this fund provide monetary assistance to the families of employees who died during the term of employment and provide expenses for domestic helpers to employees whose wives are in the hospital or to former employees who are bedridden.

It is also customary for a company to provide a wide range of training courses, not necessarily related to job content, for employees and their families—for example, flower arrangement, classic dancing, singing, and cooking. Lessons in these skills help to create a cultured, well-mannered staff.

All in all, both formal and informal affairs, official and private matters, are intermingled in Japanese organizational life. The situation symbolizes the paternalistic unity of management and worker and drives employees to new heights of achievement.

Bonus for *Bon* and the New Year

Another important practice in the reward system of the Japanese organization is the customary payment of a sizable semiannual bonus to all employees. The bonus is often equivalent to three months' regular pay, so each employee usually receives eighteen months' pay during a year's period. The bonus is usually paid early in summer for the *bon* festival and again at year-end to celebrate the coming new year.

Both periods are very festive seasons in Japanese society. The first three or even seven days of the new year are well known as the nation's biggest holidays, and *bon* is the so-called Buddhist All Souls' Day. It is said that during the *bon* festival the souls of all ancestors come back to the family domicile. Every Buddhist family is supposed to burn a welcome fire or prepare a lantern bonfire for the departed spirits of its ancestors, and then go to the cemetery and lay wreaths on the graves. Nowadays, the custom of the welcome fire and the lantern bonfire is diminishing in urban areas, but big crowds of people still visit the graveyards and lay wreaths there in summertime.

During both periods, Japan is overcome by a festive atmosphere and people take days off. In the first three to five days of the new year, almost all government offices and all companies stop their business activities, and in the *bon* period many small companies, which recruit most of their workforces from the countryside, stop production for about a week because the employees return to their hometowns to see their parents and relatives and to visit the graves of their ancestors.

The payment of a sum of money to employees on these two occasions stems from the practice of the merchant class in the Tokugawa era. The merchants and artisans took holidays only twice annually—during the *bon* festival and the New Year's celebration—and did not have Sundays off. There was no concept of a Sabbath to be observed every seven days. Accordingly, employees were given holidays and temporarily released from the daily hard work during the two seasons—the New Year and *bon*. The owner-merchant paid employees a certain amount of money as a special allowance for their home leave. This practice was particularly beneficial to the apprentices, who were not paid at all for the work but were just given lodging and food within the merchant compound. Gaining job know-how was their remuneration.

Today, in the modern industrial society, this payment of a special holiday allowance is called a "bonus." The Japanese have a popular expression, "It's like *bon* and New Year's Day coming at the same time," which they use to refer to any wonderful event or occasion. This would probably be expressed in the West as, "It's like Christmas and your birthday rolled into one." Bonus time is definitely such an occasion.

In contrast to Western firms, a Japanese company or government office pays its employees a bonus for *bon* and the New Year regardless of whether it is making a profit. Thus the bonus has become very much a part of the regular reward system. Employees expect it and organize their living standard around it. Any special purchase, such as a car or expensive furniture, is usually delayed until bonus season. Since the size of a bonus is a determining factor in department store sales and bookings at vacation resorts, the nation as a whole watches the bonus scale of industries as an exciting indicator of economic trends.

The bonus payment for each six months is the topic of extensive negotiation with the unions. While the union demands more than the total amount of money to be allotted for bonuses, management is interested in assigning specific sums to each individual with the intention of making the bonus a way of rewarding a particularly productive or energetic worker. However, in practice, no large difference exists in the amounts received by the same annual "class" of employees. Clear differences exist only between the hierarchical ranks. But the small difference within the same rank is not negligible, as noted earlier. The difference indicates the differential of appreciation by the management, and the accumulation of such small differences will bring about more favorable advancement in the future. The bonus is a regular, expected gift from the paternalistic management to its employees, but at the same time it is a notice of appreciation for individual contribution.

The Selective Retirement System

One more aspect of the compensation programs must be noted to fully understand the Japanese way of managing human resources. This is the payment of a retirement allowance. The basic aim of the retirement allowance is to reward an employee for his length of service with the company and at the same time to discourage or even penalize voluntary retirement at an early date. Apparently, the objective is to perfect the lifetime employment system.

On the other hand, the company, by discharging older workers, has to regenerate its vitality and alleviate its increased financial burden. The retirement age has thus been set at 55 years for employees in most Japanese firms. This age limit is usually strictly enforced; but when older employees are retained for some reason, they are classified as *shokutaku* (nonregular staff) and are paid less than they used to be as regular staff members. Before World War II, this retirement system functioned quite adequately: every retiree could lead a modest postretirement life on his allowance. However, the economic environment has changed greatly in the postwar period. In the affluent Japanese society of today, average longevity has increased. It was 46.9 (male) and 49.6 (female) in 1935 but surpassed Sweden to become first in the world in 1978 with averages of 73 (male) and 78.3 (female). The life expectancy of Japanese people is now reaching 80.

Inflation in currency as well as longevity made it extremely difficult for an individual to retire at 55. Thus, extension of the age limit was put forward as a serious consideration in management-labor collective bargaining. Some companies now set the age limit at 57, some at 58, and some at 60. Many others are currently revising their retirement system, and it is expected that within a few years more than half of all Japanese firms will set the retirement age limit at 60 for their employees.

Let us now look at the other side. When the first oil crisis occurred in 1973, many firms had to reduce the number of aging workers quickly, like a ship in a storm throwing its heavy freight into the sea. But, as is clear from the paternalistic nature of the

Japanese organization, management has a grave responsibility to the workers who are discharged before the end of their useful work life. It is the *giri* (social duty) of the company to make sure that the discharged worker can enjoy a secure life after leaving the company. Thus in 1973 management called for volunteers to leave the company and offered them a handsome severance allowance in addition to their regular retirement pay. Since then, quite a few companies have made voluntary retirement part of their personnel program, allowing workers to quit and get a second job at an earlier age—45, 48, 50, or whenever they choose to withdraw from the lifetime employment program. This is the selective retirement system. To avoid losing good, qualified workers, these companies maintain a counseling office which is charged with the task of persuading better employees to remain and of "patting the shoulder of" those it deems preferable for early retirement. This patting on the shoulder, *kata-tataki*, is a popular word in personnel administration and means essentially a "recommendation for retirement."

One large textile company recently introduced a selective retirement system effective from the age of 40. This is probably the lowest age that a Japanese employee can volunteer for early retirement. Management offers to these volunteers:

1. A 40 percent premium in addition to the regular retirement allowance.
2. One-year special leave granted for learning a new skill to get a new job, with 80 percent of base salary paid for the first six months and 60 percent for the next six months.
3. A tuition fee for acquiring a new skill, with up to ¥ 10,000 (approximately $450) paid monthly.

In each plant and installation of this company, management has set up a counseling office to provide consultation services to all volunteers considering a second career. The company's position is that if an employee is to make a change in his career, the earlier the better. Thus the voluntary age begins at 40.

As these developments suggest, the lifetime employment system is changing in Japan, and an adverse wind is blowing among Japanese workers. The retirement allowance system, originally set to penalize a worker for voluntary retirement, now exists to encourage early retirement. Japanese management is definitely in a transitional stage. It will have to review and revise its traditional policies and strategies—and it has the wisdom to do so.

5

THE SUCCESSFUL
ORGANIZATION MAN

The Organization Man, by William H. Whyte, Jr., clearly showed how deeply the American working class is entrapped by the organization and how workers earn salaries and wages at the price of their individual identities. But his ironical description seems to apply even more to the Japanese working class, which is so preoccupied with the feudalistic way of thinking.

A man employed by an organization will have his tiny niche in the working society. This membership acquired on employment actually means the opening up of his life, and retirement from the organization usually indicates the shutting off of his career. The organization gives every new member an opportunity to rise to the top and motivates him by putting the fragrant smell of success right under his nose. He kneels down at the opportunity and dreams of all the rich satisfactions he may gain in the future. On every payday, he tastes a little bit of sweet victory, but soon he relaxes on his small, steady income and obscures his personal identity as he takes on the mannerisms of organizational life.

His first few months on the job make him intuitive enough to sense the internal current of the organization and the implication of the faces around him. The strong demand for conformity weighs heavily on him. Of course, he is not a human ant, and he tries to cultivate his own individuality. But the strict conformity and the group-oriented climate eventually doom him to become an object to be moved around in accordance with the will of his direct supervisor and other superiors. He will gradually master the skill to play the organizational role he has been assigned. While crouching under authority and depending on the paternalistic warmth of the organization, he tries to open a door for his own advancement, and to that end he grapples with all sorts of setbacks and hindrances. He feels the strange magic power of the organization, which forces him to be either an ugly buffoon to please everyone or a capable demon to manipulate others. When he achieves a small success, he tries to share the credit with his group and hides his pride under a mask in order to prevent possible jealousy. Even so, his happiness and pride course through his body and brew another ambition for tomorrow.

As a matter of fact, from the standpoint of management, his value will be increased not by augmentation of his human virtues but by the sharpening of his ability to yield profits for the organization. Therefore, when a young man enters an organization intent on attaining sweet victory, he is likely to be molded by the organization's magic power into an organization man. Since the Japanese organization is based on the traditional concepts of duty and dependence, a young organization man cannot develop beyond certain cultural limitations. Bound by the rules of *giri* and *ninjō* of the "*on*-tract society," he grows up into the world the company wishes to establish. He works himself hard to be a successful *kaisha-ningen* (company man).

The Company Man

What qualities does a worker need to be a successful organization man in the modern samurai society? In the preceding chapters, we examined the important cultural traditions on which Japan forged its economic success. Here, we shall examine the basic rules required for a company man to forge his success in the organization.

Grasp the "Air"

In Japan, people are moved by air. They often say, "We couldn't mention it in that air, so we withdrew our point," or "The strained air filled the conference room and made everybody silent," or "Nobody could renew the traditional air of the company." Air in these expressions is the literal translation of *kūki*, and it refers to the climate or mood pervading a situation. Japanese people lie rather flat under an emotional mood and generally surrender themselves to a psychological climate.

A successful organization man, therefore, always tries to catch the "air" of the group at the beginning of any event. Whatever he attends or is engaged in, he first discerns the general tenor of the group and tries to discover the seeds of success for him to make use of. He senses the atmosphere of the place, analyzes the organizational climate, and then proceeds to deal with the subject or make his proposal. This is a ground rule for being a good organization man. For instance, in a conference, he first smells out whether others' opinions are going to bounce up for or against him. He never proceeds toward his destination until he has grasped the air correctly.

Mr. D got a job with K Trading Company when he graduated from Tokyo Fisheries College and was immediately assigned to the branch office in Las Palmas, Canary Islands. During his association with the very cheerful people there, he enjoyed a pleasant working life for three and a half years. He was not aware that the air of the Canary Islands had transformed him. When he returned to the head office in Tokyo, his personality completely changed by Las Palmas, he was not appreciated by other company members. He was frank but rough, open-hearted but outspoken, and he could not behave like a Japanese organization man. Whenever he attended a meeting, visited customers, or conducted a negotiation, he always jumped right into the subject without taking heed of the prevailing mood or the general outlook of the group. Because he no longer fit in, he had to leave the company. Now he is operating his own little shop in Las Palmas.

If you don't want to fail in the organization, like Mr. D, you must watch the climate at any business event you attend. You should express yourself carefully and adjust your words to the mood. Don't stand out from the group. However, if you want to create a different climate more favorable to your own proposal, you will need to engage in *nemawashi* (preparatory groundwork behind the scenes) and sway people to your side beforehand.

Nemawashi is an important tool for the company man. A worker's ability to engage in *nemawashi* determines how much teamwork he will get. In the Japanese organization you can't accomplish anything alone; the competition in the group-oriented climate is too fierce to achieve success on your own. Furthermore, your own resources are fairly limited, no matter how good you are. In order to survive and succeed, you must join the team under the prevailing climate and then lead the group through *nemawashi* to create a new climate. If you can create a favorable climate for your proposal and get it through, you are a successful organization man.

Be a Jack-of-All-Trades and Master of One

The world of lifetime employment is often called a lukewarm-water society. The description is apt. Everybody's destiny lies within the pool. If anyone steps out of the water, he will immediately get a fit of sneezing and catch cold. In the lukewarm-water organization, work is a mechanized, monotonous repetition of routine duties. Yet, as in the jungle, the same natural law applies: only the fittest survive.

It is true that every successful organization man has incredible patience and endurance in performing routine work. In the modern samurai organization, a very long apprenticeship—15 to 17 years or more—precedes advancement to a managerial position. After joining a company, an employee works under the close supervision of his superiors to become skilled in various tasks and to learn how to get along with superiors, peers, and (later) subordinates. The periodic transfer system and the customary practice of having all members work together in a large room give the new worker the opportunity to learn various business activities and to be a generalist. He should make good use of this casual learning experience and try hard to become a jack-of-all-trades.

"Jack-of-all-trades" may sound distasteful to an individualist, but is a very useful cog for the organization. Japanese management cherishes such a utility player and discourages tunnel vision. It will often corner a single-sighted Ph.D. into a very specific and limited area. Once confined there, he loses all chance to move up on the escalator to a managerial position even though he gets annual increments in pay. There are many examples of this in Japan.

So if you get bored with your present unvarying assignment, you are finished and will have to float in the lukewarm water. But you rarely get tired if you consider your job trout fishing and work hard at it. You can enjoy fighting your monotonous routine. Boredom is your worst enemy in the lukewarm water. If you are truly involved in your work, you will seldom become exhausted by the amount of work you do. You will become tired and irritated by the amount you do not do.

Highly successful organization men are generally no smarter or more skilled than any others. Their secret is that they know how to make good use of their limited knowledge and have accumulated a variety of daily experiences, which they then put into a composite file for use in handling any business contingency.

At the same time, the organization man needs to have a certain specialization—one area where he is great or talented. One unfortunate consequence of the seniority system, with its periodic transfers and orderly promotions, is that many people never discover what their real talents are. Someone may have experienced a taste of success because of one thing he did very well. It is tempting to assume that this fraction of success is evidence of his ability. He must be careful in making that assumption. If he likes the job better than any other job, even better than champagne or beefsteak, his assumption may be right. And if he does that job very well and with less effort than the average worker, his assumption is correct indeed. He is gifted at the job.

Every organization man must assess each task he is assigned according to these two criteria. If he can say "yes" to both, his success lies in that area. He should focus on it and polish his talent, for management will never waste such a jack-of-all-trades who is master of one.

In short, to become a successful organization man in Japan, you must take advantage of the periodic transfer system and broaden your scope so you will have the experience needed to be a versatile manager. In the meanwhile, you have to focus on your best skills and establish your forte, which will help you win even in the fiercest competition.

Don't Try to Be a Star

In the West, the word "presentation" has an important business meaning. There is the presentation of a new model to a buyer; the presentation of a sales forecast and a proposed budget to management; even the presentation by an office clerk of an official speech to other employees. In all these situations, the Western worker has to demonstrate how good and efficient he is. In order to advance, he must sell himself at business meetings, at cocktail parties, and at every other opportunity. He tries to merchandise himself by displaying his most favorable characteristics. His salesmanship determines the effectiveness of his presentation, and ultimately his advancement.

Be careful in Japan when you make a presentation. Very few Japanese will accept a showman. You may sell your product or your company as much and as hard as you like, but selling yourself is a different matter. In the feudal days, a samurai was not supposed to put his brilliance or competence on display. He was expected to remain humble. Even the merchants, whose business was selling, kept a low profile. Following this tradition, the Japanese still believe that one should be humble and self-deprecating and that selling oneself is dirty business.

However, if you do need to make a presentation of your qualities, you may sell yourself indirectly and let others buy you. For example, in Japan a newly appointed company president usually says at his first interview, "I am surprised that I have been chosen to take on such a grave responsibility. I have just reached the point in my development where I am able to follow the path established by my predecessor and I shall make the utmost effort to meet the expectations of the company." A Westerner, hearing this remark, might well ask, "If the president is not confident about carrying out his duties, why did the shareholders pick him—and why did he accept the appointment?" Of course, the new president is thoroughly qualified—he would not have been appointed otherwise. No Japanese is misled by such a remark. The people have a saying, "An able hawk wouldn't show its sharp claw." If the new company president had said, "Sure, I can take on this responsibility. I am extraordinarily experienced and qualified. I am the right person for the job," people would probably have underrated his ability. Strangely, humility is the best selling weapon in Japan.

A typical Japanese guest room has only one piece of art displayed in the *tokonoma* (alcove), even though the master of the house may have a substantial art collection. Instead of displaying all the pieces throughout the room, as is often done in the West, the Japanese host prefers to show only one special piece which represents his profound taste, or to display a different piece during each of the four seasons. In Japan, it is a tradition that an individual should not blow his own trumpet. If a person is truly capable, his performance will reveal that fact anyway, so why advertise? He should package himself subtly and show confidence without ostentation. That will give others a flash flood of impressions about him. There is no need to catalog all one's strong points and discuss them openly.

Theatrical or ostentatious behavior invites hostility in the Japanese organization. You are neither a TV talent nor a stage actor. Your performance in business must match your rank and status in the organization. Never try to make an outstanding display of yourself. When you are on the escalator, it is very rude to cut into the queue for promotion. Even if you have done your job better than anybody else, don't act like a winner. What you need for advancement is not jealousy, envy, and admiration but support, appreciation, and sympathy. You may have a confident and trustworthy manner, a quickness in responding to managers' requests, an eagerness to be helpful to others, skill in making immediate decisions, an ability to take action promptly, and a willingness to speak up clearly and decisively on every issue that arises in the organization. All these are magnificent qualities for an organization man to have. But don't show them off. Overselling is fatal to your career development. Others will become aware of your good qualities in any case, so don't try to "outsmart" them. Your success in the internal competition depends on self-control.

As noted earlier, a job in Japan is not merely a contractual arrangement for pay. It is a source of identification with a larger entity—a satisfying sense of being part of something big and significant. Naturally, *wa* (concord) is most important in this cohesive environment. If anyone violates the harmony of the group by beating his own drum too loudly, he will be excluded. Nobody can be a star in the Japanese organization.

Tactfully Communicate No Without Saying No

It is often said among foreigners that Japanese people avoid saying yes or no directly. They may understand that a person is having some difficulty answering in absolute terms and is trying to hedge and do his best to avoid giving a clear answer. They regret such an indecisive attitude. But actually the Japanese say yes very often. It is a common word in conversation. When a Japanese avoids saying yes or no clearly, it is most likely that he wishes to say no.

Then why does he hesitate to say no? Because it would hurt the feelings of those who live together with him in the close-knit vertical society. Saying no to someone else's request is usually considered rude, impolite, and uncivilized. And saying no to the requests of superiors or visitors is completely taboo. Therefore, one has to be tactful and diplomatic in conveying a negative message and must express it in an indirect and civilized manner. Foreign businessmen who do not understand this Japanese custom, or who cannot say no diplomatically at meetings or negotiation tables, are usually condemned to a bitter and costly defeat—in terms of outright rejection of their proposal, unfulfilled work orders, postponement, and so on.

The success of both the organization man and the independent businessman depends on how tactfully they can communicate no without saying it. So if you wish to be successful in Japan, you should learn some popular ways of insinuating no without coming right out and saying it. Then you will be able to meet the Japanese businessman on his own terms.

One highly recommended approach is to understand the

other party's intention and show your appreciation before you convey your negative response. For example:

"I fully understand your cordial proposition (or your particular proposal), but unfortunately I am in a different position from you and I can't help seeing the matter in another light."

Here the tone is sympathetic or halfway affirmative throughout—a far better approach than merely saying, "No, I can't agree with you." Never say no directly. It will have an undesirable echo.

Another way to avoid an outright refusal is to say, "I will consider it" or "Let me think it over." These are the words the merchants in Osaka traditionally use to imply that they cannot accept your proposal but will reconsider it if you fill the gap between them and you and come back with a better offer. The phrase "I will consider it" is actually an opening for you to adjust your proposal. It is strictly up to you to follow through or not. Such a postponement of a decision is tantamount to saying no—or perhaps, "No, but try me again."

A third approach, if you are good at humor, is to joke about the subject and laugh it off as an unimportant matter. If you can tactfully pass the whole subject off as a joke, the other party will accept your response as a no because you are not taking the matter seriously. But do it gracefully. Black humor or a tasteless joke will undo the good relationship you have established.

A fourth approach is to say, "It's a bit difficult." *Chotto* (a bit) is a significant word in Japanese business conversations and often really means "a great deal." It implies that the proposal poses great difficulty for the businessman, but he doesn't want to be embarrassed by confessing his inability to accept. This is a typical way of saving *kao* (face, or pride) in Japan and at the same time of avoiding a direct no.

The final technique is to scratch your head and emit a long drawn-out "Saaaah," which translates as "I don't know" or "I really can't agree with you."

Pick the Right Habatsu (Clique) and Stay in Touch with It

In the preceding chapter, I mentioned that nepotism plays a part in the basic recruitment process. A Japanese organization is manipulated to a surprising degree by this kind of informal relationship. Known as the *oyabun-kobun*, or parent-child relationship, it is an explicitly recognized set of reciprocal obligations between senior and junior members of a company. This informal relationship survives strongly between older and younger, superior and subordinate, and often has a heavy component of paternalism. The kinshiplike ties between *oyabun* and *kobun* are quite strong and extend beyond formal organizational lines.

For example, an *oyabun* feels more responsible for the well-being and career progress of his *kobun* than a department manager feels for the progress of his workers. His *kobun* are not necessarily within his department—his sense of responsibility goes far beyond sectional and departmental borders and even extends outside the work situation. Internal problems, informal instructions, organizational maneuvering, quarrels on a personal level, secrets of personnel administration—all these are taken care of between *oyabun* and *kobun*. Their mutual support has been and remains an important part of Japanese organizational life. Of course, the more *kobun* an *oyabun* has, the stronger he will be in the organization; and the more powerful he is, the more likely that his *kobun* will gain higher posts in the organization.

As described earlier, bright young men are recruited from a limited number of universities, which means in practice that the same annual group, on entry into the company, has usually had some previous close contact with a particular senior member of the company. In addition, graduates of the same university often become familiar with and closely associated with each other. This intimacy is maintained and developed in the company through parties, sports, and other informal activities. On the basis of such common background and interests, distinct cliques, or *habatsu*, develop that play a very important, though informal, part in career progress and success.

Employees who do not belong to any clique are overshadowed and are apt to fall off the escalator on the way to moving up from lower to higher positions. To succeed, therefore, you must be part of a clique which can look after your career progress. If possible, get into a large, powerful clique connected with the top executive who seems to have the most pull in the organization. The role of a senior member of the organization in these cliques is called *hiki* (pull or patronage). You need his pull for your advancement and he needs your support to strengthen his position. You can't achieve anything alone. There is no "do it yourself-ism" in the Japanese organization. Choose your clique carefully—pick the group that is most likely to bring you success—and stay in direct, personal contact with it at all times. Your allegiance will be very much appreciated.

Don't Be Afraid of Making Mistakes

Every year thousands of people in the organization go down the drain because of their mistakes and only a few emerge on the top of the organizational pyramid as winners.

Mr. E was a salesman employed on a permanent basis. One day he found out that his monthly base pay was ¥400 (nearly $2) less than his peers'. He immediately suspected that he had been underrated and was extremely distressed. To outsiders, a difference of ¥400 per month may be very little, and in monetary terms it is. But it mattered a great deal to Mr. E. It meant that management regarded him as less meritorious than other salesmen, and accordingly his promotion would be delayed. Finally, he went to his manager and asked for an explanation. The manager told him to recall the day when he goofed off somewhere and missed a negotiation meeting with an important customer. Even though he had been a very competent salesman, he was underrated thereafter because of his one mistake. It was a serious setback for his career.

Since the seniority-based escalator goes up gradually at the same speed, organization men of the same annual class should, in theory, be promoted to a certain managerial rank at the same time. But, as noted earlier, it does not work that way in practice. The organization does not have a sufficient number of managerial posts for all those on the slate. Naturally, personnel managers will screen people in close connection with top management. They conduct merit reviews to single out better candidates for the posts, and in the process of rating they try to eliminate ones who have fumbled in the game. Those who have made any serious mistake will be put on the negative list and, as a result, will fall off the regular track for promotion.

Once anyone gets behind his peers, he has to put in five times as much effort to catch up. So every organization man is cautious in his daily work.

However, a successful organization man is not overly cautious in carrying out his responsibilities. He knows that his capability shrinks if he becomes too nervous and afraid of making mistakes. If you avoid making mistakes at all times, you have to avoid taking risks. You can probably survive in the organization without taking chances, but you can't succeed. And certainly you won't enjoy your work.

It is risk-taking ability that separates the winner from the loser. If you always try to play it safe and rely solely on some kind of map, landmark, or other guidepost provided by other people, you just have to stagnate. You will find later that your stagnation is just as fatal to your career as an overt blunder. If you have an idea, work it out as a shiny new plan for the company's growth and present it in due course. If you are hesitant, like 90 percent of the organization men, you will never get out of your rut and join the 10 percent who are successful. The insights that come from your past experience will guide you in reading the warning signals. You can calculate each risk you face. You may have to hold back, sometimes, but all your holding back will someday help you move forward at the best possible speed.

The largest whiskey distiller in Japan offers its employees several awards, including the Greatest Confession Prize, the Highest Unpopularity Prize, the Superoptimistic Proposal Prize, and the Most Arrogant Prize. The Greatest Confession Prize is awarded to the man who confesses the greatest mistake made in the company. For instance, it might be given to a man who reports that he caused a sudden stoppage in the production line by mistake. The Highest Unpopularity Prize is given to the man who has made a speech which was most unpopular among company members. The Superoptimistic Proposal Prize goes to the man who has made the most optimistic proposal to the company. The Most Arrogant Prize is awarded to the man who has presented the most arrogant suggestion to management.

Apparently, the company is trying to encourage its members to speak up openly and not to be afraid of making mistakes. The aim of its policy is clear. Management appreciates employees' mistakes if they are caused by an enthusiastic desire to aid the company. No wonder the average sales per employee in this company is ¥160 million (approximately $727,000) annually.

Grow over Drinks on the Way Home

I heard from one Asian that in the colonial days the people of his fatherland were strictly prohibited from putting salt in their food. This policy, he said, was aimed at keeping the country a colony, for a salt deficiency causes people to lose both the will and the strength to revolt.

According to legend, a similar policy was instituted by the Tokugawa Bakufu in the rural areas of Japan during the late eighteenth century. In order to subjugate the rebellious peasants, who were the largest in population and ranked second to the samurai, the Bakufu strictly banned them from eating beef. However, the Japanese peasants were not completely subdued by this ordinance. (In fact, peasant riots broke out occasionally in those days.) After dark, the people hid behind thick bushes, made a fire, and cooked beef with some green vegetables on a *suki* (spade). This is the origin of *suki-yaki* (grilling on a spade), the world-famous Japanese dish cooked in a shallow, square iron pan in the circle of four or five people.

The Japanese working class of today has inherited not only the peasants' way of cooking beef but also their habit of eating and drinking after work. We can imagine how many people indulge in this afterwork activity if we take another look at the astonishing figures on company expenses for social activities described in Chapter 4.

Any long-standing practice in this world has some raison d'être, and the afterwork tradition does have certain merits for the organizational "peasants." The first merit is that it helps the organization man relax over drinks with friends on the way home and get rid of the mental cholesterol accumulated during the day. Unlike the contract society of the West, in which a worker can leave an employer quite easily, hollering "The hell with him," the *on*-tract society usually exhausts one's nerves with its tightly knit groups bound by the traditional concepts of *giri* (social duty) and *on* (social debt). *Sake* (rice wine) loosens the organization man's tongue, so that he can lash out at his *kachō* (section chief) and *buchō* (department head) and figuratively crush them to pieces outside of their presence. Next day, he will be fresh and work again diligently for *kachō, buchō,* and the organization. It is much like the peasants who thwarted the Tokugawa Bakufu by holding a *suki-yaki* party in the bushes after dark and then obediently went to work in the fields the next morning.

The second merit of the afterwork tradition is that it gives the organization man a chance to collect information over drinks.

Like everyone else in the company, his range of official activities is limited, and he always takes pains to watch his tongue. He needs more information about what is happening beyond the border of his working territory in order to arm himself. So he often takes or follows his company friends to a pub or tavern to exchange information with them. From the information he can figure out what's going on around him. If his leading question is superb, he can garner very useful information and thereby grow for tomorrow. Success is very expensive in the vertical organization.

Third, superiors make use of such personal, afterwork activities to develop an informal training program. Advice and instructions are often imparted to subordinates in this informal, warm atmosphere. There is good reason for this practice. Both superiors and subordinates work together, usually in a large room, and superiors can't reprimand a subordinate openly in front of other members. In order to solve a touchy problem or persuade a subordinate, the superior takes him out for a drink on the way home. Then the informal training session begins. Over drinks each can talk freely, and the superior, if he is a good communicator, can rectify misunderstandings or redirect the misguided performance of the subordinate. At the same time, he can imbue the subordinate with his own views or philosophy. This relaxed two-way communication can be very constructive, uniting subordinates behind common goals and releasing a great flow of creativity. Thus on-the-drink training is sometimes more effective than on-the-job training in Japan.

If an employee doesn't care for a drink on the way home, it is almost certain that he will be left behind in the race. As described above, a pub or tavern often serves as a clinic or information center, or even a training camp. A successful organization man grows over drinks. He doesn't hesitate to spend a little extra on his career development.

Never Fail to Consider the Mysterious Power of Women

As discussed in Chapter 3, the successful organization man owes his career progress in no small measure to his wife. In Japan, therefore, it has been the ideal of a man to marry a woman like Mrs. Kazutoyo Yamauchi of the sixteenth century, who bought her husband a very valuable horse with her savings and thereby assisted him in rising in the society. Mr. Yamauchi, a samurai of 400 *koku* (rice stipend) when married, was greatly honored with his beautiful horse and stepped up the promotional ladder to *daimyō* rapidly. Finally, he was assigned to be lord of the Tosa clan, with a stipend of 202,600 *koku*. Though his performance and achievements in the battlefield were remarkable and recognized, his outstanding career progress was credited in history to his wife. Since then, she has been esteemed by Japanese people as the exemplary wife of an organization man.

Nobody denies that a wife's assistance is indispensable to a husband's career progress. But we tend to forget the mysterious power of women in other respects. As an example, let us look at the Japanese custom of sending *chūgen* (midsummer presents) and *seibo* (year-end presents) to superiors.

Japan is a land of greetings by presents. One present is given after another, on one occasion after another. When people visit a friend in the hospital, they naturally bring him a get-well-soon present. If they go to see a departing friend off, they usually give him a small amount of money as a farewell present. Both at weddings and at funerals, every attendee is expected to grace the occasion with a present in proportion to his social status. Some presents are given in celebration of others. Some are made to help defray the considerable expense of an event, such as a wedding or a funeral. Some people expect to receive a favor in return for the visits they make and the presents they take. In any case, the Japanese are a very practical people, and the economy would sink to a considerable extent if everybody stopped giving presents as greetings.

Chūgen and *seibo* are the most popular presents in Japanese society and are given at *bon* (the midsummer Buddhists' festival) and *kure* (year-end). These presents are given from the lower echelons to the upper echelons—for example, from subcontractors to the parent company and, within the organization, from subordinates to superiors.

Chūgen and *seibo*, the so-called greetings of *bon-kure*, have a long history. When the tradition actually began is unknown, but it flourished in the Tokugawa period and became a firmly established custom. The tradition is all well and good, showing as it does the innate appreciation to a superior who performed some expected favor. In the preindustrial society, the peasants gave homemade rice cakes or hand-made wooden clogs as indications of their sincere gratefulness, but nowadays people buy handsome factory-made presents from department stores and have them gift-wrapped and delivered.

Today, *chūgen* and *seibo* are important seasonal greetings of the organization man, for they come at the time of the semiannual bonus. Thus, when the season comes, factory-made greetings pile up in the house of a VIP as evidence of his importance or the magnitude of his leadership. All are customary greetings, but they are not without diplomatic value. Intimacy invites intimacy; trust invites trust. *Chūgen* and *seibo* have thus become the seasonal lubrication for maintaining personal relationships.

Women often play an important part in this tradition. For example, when the wife of Mr. Department Head speaks very highly of Mr. X's excellent greeting item by saying, "He has a strong sense of *giri*," Mr. Department Head is sure to be impressed with Mr. X. In turn, Mr. X, with his great sense of selecting an item for Mrs. Department Head, wins the good, clean, and easy battle to get on his manager's mind.

Here is another example of a woman's mysterious power. People often say that female workers in a company are just window dressing and are not utilized to their full capacity. In

Japan this is generally true, because Japanese women prefer marriage to lifetime employment. Nevertheless, we shouldn't overlook the fact that these female workers are usually engaged in secretarial and liaison work and are therefore in close touch with managerial personnel. Very often they are information messengers. Secrets of workers and internal affairs often slip out of their mouths while they are working around section chiefs and department heads. Their role as emotional propagandists should not be underestimated.

Unfortunately, the mysterious power of women is undervalued in Japan, which has a strong tradition of male supremacy inherited from feudalism and Confucian concepts. But the truth is that Japanese women have as much strength of will and are just as brave as men; they may even possess greater will power and psychological strength than men. They just reserve their powers within.

Be an Expert at Haragei

A homogeneous group of people who speak the same language might naturally be expected to be highly communicative. However, in this enclosed island society, where personal relationships are emotionally delicate, people are liable to hold their tongues or speak in a roundabout way and imply their intentions rather than communicate them directly. Everyone in Japan expects the other person to understand the whole thing by hearing only a small part of it.

This is particularly true in business. Many businessmen will express themselves clearly in sports or other activities but will restrain themselves when it comes to talking about serious business matters. In communications between superior and subordinate in particular, people are not likely to unfold everything on their minds. The person in a lower position, therefore, is likely to fail to respond properly unless he reads the mind of his superior correctly.

Many a Japanese bows without reason, smiles meaning-lessly at times, and uses ambiguous words often in conversation. All these actions are designed to disguise his own intention until he has read the other person's mind correctly and thus gained an advantageous position in the exchange of words. The Tokugawa style still prevails in Japan.

This sort of *haragei* (intuitive communication) takes place in the *ringi* decision-making system described in Chapter 4. The system itself is good insofar as it utilizes the abilities of the younger organization men at the bottom. But to obtain final approval at the top, the planner has to prepare a *ringisho* care-fully so as to get it through the necessary channels and obtain acceptance at every checkpoint. His proposal must be stated in diplomatic language of the highest degree, or in words slippery as an eel, if it is to get through and must not clash with the interests of upper echelons. The proposal can never be baldly frank. To prevent rejection, the planner uses vague words. In Japan, such a statement is said to be as irridescently colored as silk fabric *(tamamushi-iro)*.

At the same time, the proposal must be stated as the planner actually intended it to be. He has to push through his real plan. He must make certain that others read his mind correctly and understand his real intent. These two efforts might seem to contradict each other, but the Japanese never see any potential conflict in this type of communication. Their *haragei* just does away with the contradiction.

In Japan, people speak very highly of a man who wins in grand *haragei*. Without telling others what he is really thinking, he makes them follow his lead and reach the destination he wants. Defeat is usually caused by a breakdown in *haragei*. Anyone who contributes to such a breakdown in the organization ought to think twice about what it is costing. And he ought to be on guard for the backlash. There are two requirements for successful business communication: the first is to read others' intentions more quickly than they read yours, and the second is not to expose your own intention until others grasp it, so that by implication you sway them to your point of view. Anyone who can neither read another person's mind nor let the other person read his mind is not worth a damn in Japan.

Here is the typical jargon of Japanese bureaucrats: "We will look ahead and think it over." This sounds as if they are going to consider the proposal and move forward to realize it. But in most cases they don't move forward. They do look ahead and consider it, but in vain. What they actually mean by the jargon is "It is very difficult and seems impractical," or "We will study it but won't be able to do it." This is another *haragei* to avoid saying no. Japanese bureaucrats also often say, "We would like to try all possible means to solve this problem in a manner acceptable to both you and us." This also sounds very positive, but it will be very time-consuming as the two parties try to reach a point of agreement. The expert at *haragei*, while tactfully concealing his real intention (for instance, to say no), sustains the other person's position and manipulates his mind.

Haragei is the communication of *ishin-denshin* (conveyance from mind to mind) and is based on tacit understanding. How someone reads your mind is completely left to him. You can't confirm his understanding. If you confirm it, the communication is no longer *haragei*. Furthermore, you will be devaluated and labeled "importunate and stubborn" if you do confirm or reconfirm what someone else attributes as your meaning. And if you fail to read the mind of your superior, he will surely lament your ability by saying, "What a weak little fellow!" instead of regretting his own improper and insufficient words. He may even get angry at your being unable to grasp his meaning completely.

Haragei is not based on any systematic logic, and you can't use X-ray to see through someone else's mind. You just have to read his mind in whatever way you tend to read. The comprehension will vary. When the situation changes, your understanding of his intention and the conclusion you draw may change as well.

Perhaps the superior himself may alter his intention when the situation fades away. The organization man, in order to read the superior's mind correctly, must always be ready to adjust his response according to the circumstances. There is always uncertainty in *haragei*. It is a gamble of communication. Success is achieved by the person who develops both the offensive ability to read others' minds and the defensive ability to keep his intention from being read. In other words, your success or failure will be determined by your ability to perform *haragei*. The tradition is a carryover from the samurai society, when vassals fought furiously through *haragei*. It is for this reason that *Chushingura* (the story of 47 samurai's revenge)—a grand drama of typical *haragei*—never loses its popularity in Japan.

Don't Kill the Problem, Solve It

We can make a good guess at how successful an organization man will be if we know what his problems are and how he solves them. For example, he will be unlikely to succeed if:

- He creates problems that he cannot handle.
- He has problems that he is not aware of.
- His problems involve people in positions of power higher than his own.

On the other hand, he will have a good chance to succeed if:

- He is able to solve his problems without inviting other people's anger.
- He never fails to compromise with others in solving problems.

What this boils down to is that we can judge the prospects of an organization man not only by his position in the company but by the way he handles his problems.

It is virtually impossible to accomplish anything worthwhile in this world without running across problems. People who work in an organization face a never-ending series of forks along the road. They may get puzzled at the crossroads, or be unable to find a shortcut. They may have to give up their chances of success. They will face difficulties and problems here and there.

Although a person needs a kind of bulldozing power to break the impasse of a problem, he must also have bargaining power to settle the problem. He should make sure that his problem-solving plan contains lots of flexible measures. It must not be narrow and confining. Owing to the traditional code of *wa* (harmony), the Japanese people generally dislike doing away with the problem by force. They usually look for the point at which they can compromise in solving the problem and reach a solution that satisfies all parties.

In the emotionally charged Japanese society, it is generally advisable to solve the problem by adopting an emotional approach. This doesn't mean using intuition or being self-centered. Rather, it means being sensitive to the feelings of others. For example, there were two characters in one company—one was Mr. Takagi, head of the accounting section, and the other was Mr. Moto, a member of the sales department. Takagi was mean and nasty just because he was very sharp at accounting and very capable at finding others' mistakes in documents. Nobody liked him. In contrast, Moto was good-natured but a little dull, and weak in handling figures. Takagi often discovered Moto's mistakes on various sales reports and tormented him painfully. But Moto never hesitated to visit Takagi's desk with the documents, for he wanted to solve his problems and learn from the expert. At session after session, Moto would listen to Takagi's disparaging remarks. Then he devised an invaluable means of pacifying the accountant's irritable temper. He had only to make a pun once in a while during the session. Takagi could not help grinning, and sometimes laughed loudly with Moto. By dissolving the first problem with Takagi, Moto was able to discuss the subject matter fully and learn the ropes of advanced accounting. Thus he overcame his weak points within a few months and never again created a problem in documenting sales figures. He is now the manager of a branch office overseas.

In a Japanese organization, workers knock heads constantly, clashing in their ambitious attempts to outsmart each other. Underneath the veneer of politeness and allegiance, the tough muscle of basic motives and desperate tactics is laid bare. Problems are inevitable. You can't work up to full capacity or grow to your full potential if you run away from problems. Certainly problems are costly and even dangerous sometimes, but if you handle them properly they also give you a chance to build up your muscle and thereby earn big rewards in prestigious areas.

When a person encounters a problem, he naturally tries to solve it as quickly as possible. Often, he approaches it too hastily and ends up killing it. A man of short temper, a type often seen among able managers, is especially likely to kill his problem instead of dealing carefully with it. Like a cowboy in an American movie, his solution is to shoot down his enemy on the spot without negotiating. One shot, "Bang!" is quite enough to straighten out the problem—he thinks. However, this kind of combat does not solve his problem. Any problem disposed of by ruthless efficiency simply creates another problem in its wake. For instance, if you kill a tax problem by using false figures, another problem, a bigger one this time, will certainly come your way later from the tax office. As long as the problem is there, you can't kill it completely. The ghost of the problem will resurrect from the dead and knock on your door. You will be in deeper trouble.

Even more important, you will make enemies if you try to kill the problem and fail. Dishonest dealings with problems inevitably invite hostility. How many people, sections, or companies despise each other because one (or both) was lied to or cheated on? Human beings are sensitive animals. In the *on*-tract society, people are burdened with the weights of *giri* (social duty) and *on* (social debt). Damaging someone's *kao* (pride) by killing the problem is enough to crystallize his hostility. It is virtually essential to be diplomatic in solving a problem within and outside the organization. Threats may be good weapons for killing a problem, but they don't solve it to your heart's content.

If you caused a problem in the first place, or helped to cause it, you should have the power to correct it. A successful organization man always removes the reason for his involvement in a problem. He treats the problem tactfully and meets the requirements for solution with a smile. If he is patient and acts sensibly, he will win.

Japanese Leadership

From among the successful organization men a brilliant leader emerges, and the leader is living testimony to the power and dignity of the organization. He sheds his rays on his subordinates, so the light of the organizational philosophy illuminates their productive path and steers the company's social and political institutions. Very frequently his leadership is unuttered and unwritten, possessing all the more power to organize people toward a common goal.

Historians and writers have described a number of general qualities required for leadership. Here, I will take up only the unique qualities of Japanese leadership, inherited from earliest times. It is a flower no less indigenous to the soil of Japan.

The first proviso of a Japanese leader is the ability to appear to be unaware of what's going on while actually being in complete command of the situation. This is an unusual quality in a leader, but there was one man who fit the description exactly. It was the artillery officer Yasuke Ōyama (later known as General Iwao Ōyama), who developed the Yasuke artillery gun during the

Meiji era (1868–1913). When Ōyama became supreme commander of the army in the Russo-Japanese War (1904), the main weapons that were defeating the Russian troops were those Yasuke guns. But Ōyama did not talk about guns or soldiers and never asked his officers what was going on. He simply created a climate that encourged his officers to use their abilities and to get the maximum performance from their men.

This quality is extremely valuable in Japan. The leaders of Japan's vertical society have come up from the bottom, and have climbed up with much effort. They have wide experience and expertise in several fields. However, even though a leader knows a great deal about many things, he is careful not to instruct his followers in how to do every little task. If he did, his followers would lose their sense of responsibility and refuse to take action on their own or to cooperate fully with his injunctions. Although Japan is often said to be a nonindividualistic society, a leader who ignores individual ability and tries to suppress individual initiative cannot succeed. Acting as if one is not aware of what is going on is one way to encourage subordinates to rely on their own abilities and to demonstrate their loyalty. The successful leader in Japan's group-oriented society is the one who can activate the group's energies to the fullest, reserving only the final decision-making power for himself.

What a sharp contrast this is to the self-expression expected of both leaders and followers in the West. The leader in the West wishes to demonstrate his own "personal style" to his followers, telling them, in effect, "I'm not just the ordinary sort of boss." He tries to show that he does things with flair, in his own way, and produces distinctive results. As everyone knows, when the American presidency changes hands, all the important government posts change hands too. In order to carry out his own policies, the new President chooses people for the cabinet and advisory posts from the worlds of government, business, journalism, and so on. He assembles talents that can assist him in producing the results he desires, and in reaching the goals he has set for his administration. In contrast, when the Japanese Prime Minister forms a new cabinet, he searches for consensus on matters, rather than trying to impose his will on the group. The secret of remaining in power for a long time in Japan is to subjugate one's individuality to the group. A good leader never pretends to be a capable talent.

The second proviso for leadership in Japan is the ability to assist one's subordinates in their upward climb to success. Those who have the means and ability to help their followers up the ladder are the ones who come to power, and once there, stay in power.

Among a group of, say, 100 workers who entered the organization in the same year, only ten or so will move up to the position of department head; a few will eventually succeed to the director's level; and after 30 years or so, only one will finally reach the top—the position of company president. This competition for rank transcends distinctions in types of work and is particularly fierce between white-collar workers with similar educational backgrounds. One reason is that employment in Japan is centered around a particular company rather than around a profession or a specific line of work. The usual practice is to have an employee move from one sort of job to another within the company throughout his career. This weakens the "horizontal" concept—specialization of job—and strengthens the "vertical" concept—rank. The leader who can extend his hand down to his subordinates and give them a hike up the ladder gathers the most followers and, with their support, finally reaches the seat of power himself.

Japan is a "give and take" society in which giving and returning gifts are of central importance. People are always receiving gifts, having things done for them, and then doing something in return. This "something in return" is known as *okaeshi*. The person who ignores *okaeshi* will be judged in violation of the rules of *giri* and *ninjō* and will find himself excluded from the group.

The truth of this is evident from the lives of Japan's medieval samurai leaders, and from the plays and dramas set in Japan's Turbulent Age (1467–1575). In those times, leaders who were able to distribute generous rewards for service rendered increased their followership and extended their power. This spirit is still very much alive in contemporary Japan.

Those who are able to hold the doors open to advancement for their followers receive wholehearted support and advance themselves to the heights. Protection invites support, and generosity is supported by the virtue of loyalty. Both flourish together. As a result of this practice, an elderly man with little ability, or greatly weakened faculties, who would never be chosen as a leader in the strict merit system often finds himself in a glorious public role with an impressive title. This is not really because of the traditional Japanese respect for the aged; rather, it derives from the social power the elderly leader has acquired through the close relationships he has established with numerous subordinates during his long career. With the support of these now powerful subordinates, he is pushed up to the top of the heap. This pattern is true not only in the industrial world, but also in the government bureaucracy, in the underworld, and even in fishermen's guilds.

The third proviso for leadership, related to the second, is the ability to place your trusted followers about you skillfully, forming a protective wall around yourself. No candidate for top leadership can hold the gate for promotion open equally to all his followers. He must select certain supporters who have ability and will provide him with faithful service, and attach their fortunes to his own cause. This means, of course, that he must form his own faction. All others who are candidates for top leadership are also forming and nourishing their own factions.

The main leader controls the entire factional group through the leaders of various subgroups. These subgroup leaders are the "wall" or "moat" of the main leader, and the workers are stones to be used in building the wall or moat. The strength or weakness of the main leader is determined by the positioning of these individual "stones" in his "castle wall." The subgroup leaders all give their support to the main leaders and have a considerable voice in matters of concern to the organization. Since these subgroup leaders must also represent the demands and rights of the group members they lead, conflicts of interest can sometimes result. The main leader must have the skill to maintain good relationships with the various subgroup leaders. If he fails, the wall he has built will come tumbling down.

Occasionally, a "dictatorial-type" leader appears from within the group. Since he is the dominant representative of his faction, it would seem that the balance of power in the group has swung radically to his favor. But in fact, he too must spend a considerable amount of time and energy maintaining good relations with the group. The emotional framework on which human relationships are built disintegrates easily if it is not constantly attended to. The disintegration of relationships ultimately results in the disintegration of the power bloc as well.

In my observation, leaders in certain foreign nations prefer not to have capable men as their subleaders. This is not simply a fear of criticism, but a more primal fear of being stabbed in the back. Such leaders tend to place yes-men around them as direct subordinates and try to carry out their policies on their own, using these yes-men only as decorative defense. But as a rule, yes-men lack ability, and the leader has to do everything himself. In Japan, the opposite is often true: the subordinates are exhausted protecting the boss.

The fourth proviso of a Japanese leader is the skill to instruct subordinates without putting the instructions into words. In other words, he should have the mysterious power to convey his instructions through voiceless communication.

I learned about one leader who had this quality from a short memoir which appeared in the *Nihon Keizai Shimbun* (October 23, 1980). It was the summer of 1941. The Japanese garrison forces had made peaceful inroads into French Indochina (present Vietnam). The troop leader, a second lieutenant, and his 200 soldiers were stationed at Hanoi Airport. The soldiers were permitted to leave the camp only during the daytime, but to their disappointment all the shops downtown were closed in the day because of the burning heat. Since the shops were open only in the evening, the soldiers could enjoy nothing. Then the lieutenant, in sympathy with his men, issued a special, arbitrary order at his own risk permitting the soldiers to go out in the evening. Leaping with joy, the soldiers rushed into the amusement district. There they saw one foreign officer treating a native man cruelly. They became enraged at the officer's inhumane act and immediately beat him up. The incident became a big issue between the Japanese and the foreign troops, and Major Kato, commander of the Japanese garrison, had to deal with the problem.

Later, Major Kato summoned the lieutenant to his room. The lieutenant stood before the major's desk, anticipating thunder and severe punishment, but the major simply glanced at the lieutenant and went on reading his official documents. He never once looked up at the lieutenant, acting as if he had completely forgotten the man. Ten minutes, twenty minutes, nearly thirty minutes passed. The lieutenant remained at attention during all this time. Then Major Kato abruptly looked up at the lieutenant and asked in a dignified voice:

"Do you know why you are summoned here?"

"Yes, sir!"

Kato looked damned hard into the lieutenant's face. After a brief pause, he said, "All right, go back!"

"Yes, sir!" The lieutenant returned.

Years later, the lieutenant recalled that dreadful day and described it in his memoir. "I was so shocked at the time," he wrote, "it was like my heart had been stung by a needle."

There was no actual instruction from Major Kato. Nothing at

all. Yet the lieutenant was thoroughly instructed and corrected. (Major Kato was later killed in an air battle while leading the famous Kato Falcon Fighters.)

Here is another illustration of wordless instruction. A certain section chief was transferred to a smaller section in a Japanese company. The move was known to everybody as a demotion. He was extremely discouraged by this personnel action and decided to make an appeal to the director, whom he knew very well.

When he visited the director's house, he was ushered into the drawing room, where he was served a cup of Japanese green tea. Left alone with the tea, he waited and waited, but the director did not appear. As he waited, he grew impatient and began to glance about the room. He turned his eyes to the scroll hanging in the alcove. It was a beautiful calligraphy expressing "endurance." He felt at that moment as if the word picture was gazing down at him. It was like an electric shock. He was suddenly awakened by the meaning of the scroll.

When the director came into the room, the man's mind had already been made up. He made no appeal. They exchanged a few words on general matters. He felt refreshed when he left the director's house. After this visit, all his time, energy, and thoughts were redirected to his new job in the smaller section.

This is how a Japanese leader teaches others without saying a word.

In summary, the unique qualities of leadership in Japan are:

- Pretending ignorance, while delegating responsibility to subordinates.
- Rewarding subordinates with advancement for service rendered.
- Building strong factional support.
- Influencing others with voiceless instructions.

We can sum up these qualities into one neat phrase: "delegation of authority." A true leader, rather than expressing his own wishes, delegates his power, thereby giving his subordinates a sense of importance. The Japanese have established a modern bureaucratic society, but the old words of the feudal lord to his vassals still apply: *"Yoki ni hakarae"* ("Do as you see fit"). The Japanese organization depends on this spirit of delegation for its success.

Nonetheless, this sort of leadership can be very difficult to administer. Only a person who combines the charismatic qualities admired in the Orient and the pragmatism demanded in the Occident can succeed. The members of a group, though superficially suppressing their personalities, are always seeking satisfaction of their self-interests. Self-satisfaction in a vertical society is achieved by coming closer to power and authority, or attaining just a bit more power and authority than one's position deserves. From below, authority is the goal. From above, it is the source of motivation. A successful leader is one who motivates others effectively.

BIBLIOGRAPHICAL NOTE

I wish to note that I used my earlier works, *Watakushi no Kozo (Anatomy of the Self)* and *Fufu no Kozo (Anatomy of a Married Couple)*, published in Japan by PHP Institute in 1979 and 1980 respectively, for much of the material that appears in Chapter 2 and 3.

I also relied on the following books as references in order to confirm the historical record and the facts, the opinions and observations of others, and my own store of knowledge and experience.

Benedict, Ruth. *The Chrysanthemum and the Sword.* Translated as *Kiku to Katana* by M. Hasegawa. Tokyo: Shakai Shiso-sha, 1967.

Doi, Takeo. *Amae no Kozo (Anatomy of Dependence).* Tokyo: Kobundo, 1971.

Getty, J. Paul. *How to Be Rich.* London: W. H. Allen, 1966.

Hall, John W. *Japan: From Prehistory to Modern Times.* Translated as *Nihon no Rekishi* by T. Onabe. Tokyo: Kodan-sha, 1970.

Hazama, Hiroshi. *Nippon-teki Keiei (Japanese Management),* Tokyo: Nihon Keizai Shimbun-sha, 1971.

Inoue, Kiyoshi. *Nihon no Rekishi (History of Japan).* Tokyo: Iwanami Shoten, 1963.

Katoh, Kyoh. *Hidden Beauty of Japan.* Kamakura: Eiko Co., 1964.

Kuki, Shuzo. *Iki no Kozo (Anatomy of Iki).* Tokyo: Iwanami Shoten, 1930.

Milward, Peter. *Oddities in Modern Japan.* Tokyo: Hokuseido Press, 1980.

Miyamoto, Mataji, and Keiichiro Nakagawa. *Nihon Keieishi Koza (History of Business Management in Japan),* Volumes 1 through 6. Tokyo: Nihon Keizai Shimbun-sha, 1977.

Moore, Charles A. *The Japanese Mind.* Tokyo: Charles E. Tuttle Co., 1973.

Nakane, Chie. *Tate-shakai no Ningen Kankei (Japanese Society).* Tokoyo: Kodan-sha, 1972.

Nakane, Chie. *Tate-shakai no Rikigaku (Dynamics of a Vertical Society)*. Tokyo: Kodan-sha, 1978.

Nitobe, Inazo. *Bushido*. Tokyo: Charles E. Tuttle Co., 1969.

Reischauer, Edwin O. *Japan*. Tokyo: Charles E. Tuttle Co., 1964.

Reischauer, Edwin O. *The Japanese*. Tokyo: Charles E. Tuttle Co., 1973.

Sansom, George B. *Japan in World History*. Tokyo: Charles E. Tuttle Co., 1977.

Shinoda, Yujiro. *Shimaguni to Nipponjin (The Japanese and Their Island Country)*. Tokyo: Kobun-sha, 1979.

Woronoff, Jon. *Japan*. Tokyo: Lotus Press Ltd., 1979.

INDEX

Abe family, 18-19
ability, 86-87
   education and, 150
   persistence and, 85
   promotion and, 83-84
advancement
   cliques and, 193
   favoritism and, 83-84
   leaders' fostering of, 208-209
   as seniority-based, 149-150,
     152-153
age, as advancement criterion,
   149-153
Ainu people, 1-2, 18
Alvarez, Everett, 100-101
amakudari, 40-41
amorousness (*iki*), 111-114
Analects of the Nabeshima Clan, 8
anata (you), 117-118
Anatomy of Iki (Kuki), 112
ancestor worship
   in *bon* festival, 176-177
   in Buddhism, 21-22
   in business, 26-27
   Christianity and, 23, 26
   marriage and, 106-108
   in Shinto, 17-20
aotagari (preliminary recruitment), 157-158
apprenticeship, 165, 186

Army, Japanese
   after World War II, *see* Self-
     Defense Forces
   before World War II, *see* Impe-
     rial Army
arranged marriage, 104-106
authority, 99

Bell, Daniel, 63
Benedict, Ruth, 65
Bible, 22
bon festival, 176-178, 199
bonuses, 176-178
Buddhism, 6, 17, 62, 176-177
bushidō (devotion of samurai), 8,
   108
business
   benefits offered by, 174-176
   bonuses paid by, 176-178
   climate of, understanding, 184-
     185
   cliques in, 192-193
   companyism and, 95-97
   giri-ninjō in, 90-92
   hierarchy in, 32-33
   humility in, 188-190
   husband's neglect of wife for,
     126-129
   loyalty to, 65
   "no" in, 190-191

217

emotion in, 116-117
"I" in, 45-46
politeness in, 84
"yes" and "no" in, 31, 190-191
"you" in, 117-118
see also communication
layoffs, 151-152
volunteers for, 148-149
leadership quality(s), 213
advancement fostered in subordinates as, 208-209
faction building as, 209-210
influence by voiceless instruction as, 210-212
responsibility delegation as, 206-208
lifetime employment system, 48, 61-62, 96, 145-149
retirement from, *see* retirement
seniority and, 150-151
Lincoln, Abraham, 50
loans, from company, 175
loneliness, 73-75
loyalty
to army, 80-82
to business, 65, 129, 149
to group, 78-79, 92, 148
of samurai, 123, 146
to two bosses, 82-84
of workers, loss of, 96

management, 139-140, 148-149
consensus by, procedure for, 171-174
paternalism of, 140-145, 169
social expenses of, 169-171
see also chō (title of "chief");
leadership quality(s)
marriage
ancestors and, 106-107

arranged type of, 104-106
communication in, 118-120
conjugal relations in, *see* sexuality
dependence in, 136-137
language and, 116-117
polygamous type of, 102-103
see also husband; wife
Matsushita, Konosuke, 147
Matsushita Electric, 147
mechanization, 76-77
medetai (felicitations), 70-71
Meiji Restoration, 19, 25, 30, 54, 146
industrialization in, 38-40
Westernization and, 36-37
meishi (calling card), 33
merit-rating system, 164-166
mieppari (self-display), 58-60
Minamoto clan, 19
Mishima, Yukio, 55
mistakes, 193-195
MITI (Ministry of International Trade and Industry), 38, 40
Mitsubishi, 39, 47, 95
Mitsui, 39, 47, 95
monarchy, 2-4
money, as motivator, 144-145
mura-hachibu (social ostracism), 58

Nagasaki, 24
naivete (*omedetai*), 72
Nakane, Chie, 32, 88-89
nationalism, 95
National Railway, 95
nemawashi (groundwork), 172-173, 185
nepotism, 158-159, 192
New Employees Orientation Pro-